A NIGHT AT THE
PICTURES
Ten Decades of British Film

STILLS ON FRONT COVER

Laurence Olivier and Vivien Leigh in
FIRE OVER ENGLAND (1937),
directed by William K. Howard.

Celia Johnson and Trevor Howard in
BRIEF ENCOUNTER (1945),
directed by David Lean.

James Mason and Margaret Lockwood in
THE WICKED LADY (1945),
directed by Leslie Arliss.

Kay Kendall, Kenneth More, John Gregson and Dinah Sheridan in
GENEVIEVE (1953),
directed by Henry Cornelius.

Jim Dale, Kenneth Williams and Kenneth Connor in
CARRY ON CLEO (1964),
directed by Gerald Thomas.

Ben Kingsley in
GANDHI (1983),
directed by Sir Richard Attenborough.

Dr. Haing S. Ngor in
THE KILLING FIELDS (1984),
directed by Roland Joffé.

Dame Peggy Ashcroft in
A PASSAGE TO INDIA (1985),
directed by David Lean.

(FROM THE JOEL FINLER COLLECTION)

THE BEST OF BRITISH FILM MUSIC
Filmtrax double album, cassette and
compact disc available from London Records.
WINNERS: *A Video Tribute to the
very best of British Film and Music*
Video available from Polygram Video.

A NIGHT AT THE PICTURES
Ten Decades of British Film

GILBERT ADAIR and NICK RODDICK

COLUMBUS BOOKS
in association with
THE BRITISH FILM YEAR, LONDON

FIRST PUBLISHED IN GREAT BRITAIN IN 1985 BY COLUMBUS BOOKS
DEVONSHIRE HOUSE, 29 ELMFIELD ROAD, BROMLEY, KENT BR1 1LT

© MEDUSA PUBLISHING COMPANY LIMITED 1985
except:
THE BRITISH TRADITION
© GILBERT ADAIR
THE BRITISH REVIVAL
© NICK RODDICK

EDITED BY FENELLA GREENFIELD
ADDITIONAL CONTRIBUTIONS FROM SARAH JONES, NICK KENT
and CHRIS GOODWIN
CARTOONS BY ALAN PARKER

TYPESETTING BY LONDON COMPOSITION LTD.
PRINTED IN ENGLAND BY JARROLDS OF NORWICH

BRITISH LIBRARY CATALOGUING IN PUBLICATION DATA
A NIGHT AT THE PICTURES: Ten Decades of British Film
1. Moving-picture industry – Great Britain – History
I. British Film Year
384'.8'0941   HD9999.M663G7
ISBN 0-86287-188-3

ALL ILLUSTRATIONS IN THIS BOOK, UNLESS OTHERWISE CREDITED,
COME FROM THE NATIONAL FILM ARCHIVE OF THE BRITISH FILM
INSTITUTE. OUR GRATEFUL THANKS TO THE STILLS DEPARTMENT
WHO KINDLY OFFERED ADVICE AND HELP IN THE PICTURE
RESEARCH OF THIS BOOK. THEIR WORK OVER FIFTY YEARS IN
TRACKING DOWN BOTH DOCUMENTATION AND ILLUSTRATIONS OF
BRITISH FILMS HAS RESULTED IN AN INVALUABLE SOURCE OF BOTH
REFERENCE AND INSPIRATION. THE BRITISH FILM INSTITUTE HAS
BEEN AN IMPORTANT CONTRIBUTOR TO THE RECENT
REASSESSMENT OF BRITISH FILM NOT ONLY IN TERMS OF ITS
ARTISTIC MERIT BUT ALSO ITS CULTURAL AND SOCIAL IMPACT.

CONTENTS

FOREWORD by David Puttnam 7

INTRODUCTION by Sir Richard Attenborough 8

PART ONE:
THE BRITISH TRADITION
by Gilbert Adair 12

PART TWO:
THE BRITISH REVIVAL
by Nick Roddick 74

PART THREE:
THE BRITISH PICTURE 114

CRITICS' CHOICE 140

BRITISH FILM YEAR COMMITTEE 144

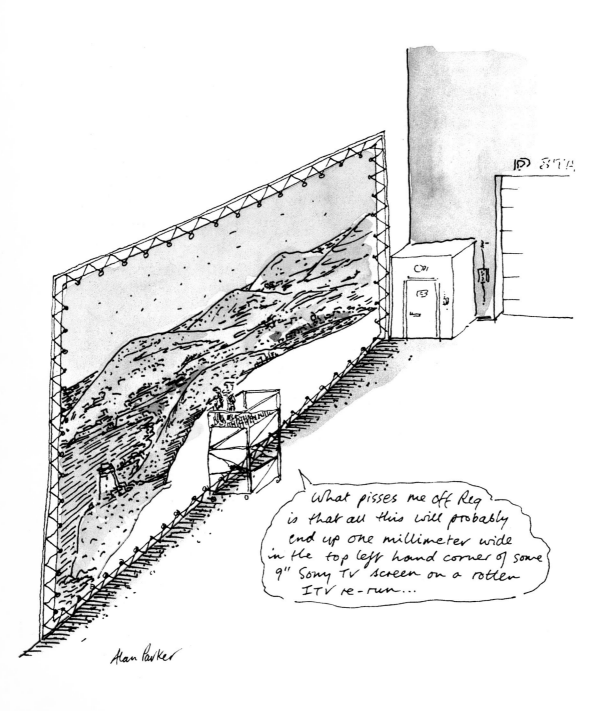

FOREWORD

The film industry, like many other British industries, has suffered chronically from this country's cherished and dangerous belief that commercial success is vulgar, that film-makers who produce successful, accessible films should somehow feel embarrassed. There are, unfortunately, all too many highbrow British film critics who set forth esoteric standards that only serve to confuse some of our most talented and creative film-makers. Writers, wishing to be perceived as 'culturally respectable', are pressured into producing inaccessible, impenetrable work which reaches a narrow audience but conforms to the fashionable critical ethos. To me, this violates the artist's instincts as surely as do any of the demands of the commercial sector, and only when critics appreciate this will the authentic social and artistic role of the cinema in our culture emerge.

British Film Year is a renewal of our commitment to our audience, in part by making the cinema a more attractive place to go. The time, effort and energy that goes into the creation of a perfect picture is lost – sometimes totally lost – when that film is viewed in any other medium. We therefore have a professional duty to encourage people to see films in the way that they were made to be seen – on large screens, with excellent sound systems and in clean, comfortable cinemas.

British cinema cannot exist without addressing large audiences, for they are the lifeblood of our industry. Critics' choices are well and good, but it is by the audience's choices that we live or die.

DAVID PUTTNAM

INTRODUCTION

British Film Year, which began on March 18, 1985, with the Royal Film Performance premiere of David Lean's *A Passage To India,* has essentially two aims.

The first is to celebrate a new era in our country's long and sometimes somewhat chequered history of movie making and to highlight one of Britain's greatest assets: our unmatched wealth of talent, skills and facilities.

The second aim of British Film Year is encapsulated in our slogan: Cinema, the best place to see films.

After the Second World War, during the late Forties and early Fifties, a night out at the cinema, 'going to the flicks' as we used to call it, was a national pastime. People went not just once, but two and three times a week. After the blackout, the dangers, the drabness and rationing which didn't end completely until 1954, cinemas were magical places. They were glamourous places too, incorporating lavish architectural flights of fancy owing a great deal to oriental palaces and temples. The staff included usherettes who showed each patron to his or her seat by torchlight, a doorman, resplendent in a uniform that wouldn't have shamed a general in some Ruritanian army and a manager who stood in the foyer to greet you, dressed, after dark, in black tie and dinner jacket. And this was in every high street up and down the country.

It seems strange, now, to recall these people and these surroundings which my generation took so much for granted and realise that, today, anyone under the age of forty will find them somewhat unbelievable.

But it wasn't the gilded pillars, or even the friendly service that kept us going to the cinema week after week. Neither was it simply the admission price which, in relation to earnings then, was eminently affordable.

We went because, as a nation, we were passionately interested in films, and the films we made were great. They reflected not only life as we knew it – in a documentary style that evolved from the war and the immediacy of newsreels – but also a fantasy life and a type of humour to which we could relate because they were rooted in our British psyche.

What happened to all this? Why did cinema admissions which stood at 1,352 million a year on average in the Fifties, drop to 338 million in the Sixties, 136 million in the Seventies and slump last year to an all time low of 55 million?

Television is, of course, the easiest culprit to blame. The number of licensed sets jumped from just under a million and a half in 1952 to just over sixteen and a half million by 1972.

What is interesting is that today, when the television companies want to attract maximum audiences over one of the big public holidays, their best bet is a famous and highly popular movie. And they have only become famous and popular for one reason – theatrical exhibition. In other words, by being screened in cinemas. The same factor is, of course, what prompts people to buy or rent films recorded on video tapes.

The truth is that even today, when many cinemas can justly be accused of being dirty, unfriendly and pretty expensive, they still have a magic that is unique. Cinema is not only the best place to see a film. Films are made to be shown in cinemas. On a big screen. As a communal activity, in which a whole audience participates together.

Those of us involved in British Film Year – and, hearteningly, we represent every segment and every faction of our industry, even those who – until now – have historically viewed each other as archrivals – are determined to revive cinema-going as a national habit. Our job is to persuade those who have abandoned it, to return, and to introduce the habit to the young.

To this end, supported by the Government, the industry has put up, in cash and in kind, £1,500,000. In addition, during the course of British Film Year, the country's three principal exhibitors, Thorn EMI, Rank and Cannon have pledged to spend £1,000,000 a month on modernising and refurbishing their cinema chains.

By the end of the year, we aim not only to have halted the downward spiral of admission figures, but to have created a positive upturn of at least four per cent. There is no reason why this cannot be achieved. In other countries it has already happened. Take the United States, for example. There, the trend was downward like ours until 1980. Today, with 90 per cent of American cinemas less than ten years old, audience figures have risen from 1,021.5 million five years ago to the current level of over 1,175 million. In France, from an all time low in 1977, admissions rose to 197 million in 1983, topping Japan by 27 million, and making her the second biggest market in the world.

How are we going to achieve a similar result? One of our first priorities is to eradicate the impression that the glitter and glamour of movies is the exclusive prerogative of London. To this end, regional committees have been set up all over the country, bringing together influential groups of people who care about cinema-going and about films on every possible level. Competing managers are, for the first time, collaborating with each other and with the media, local government, educationalists, film clubs and chambers of commerce. Between May and October 1985, our travelling roadshow, accompanied by stars and by working film technicians demonstrating their skills, will visit 25 cities and be within the reach of half the population of the United Kingdom. A winter and spring schedule, now being put together, will cover a further 30 towns and cities, with another 50 centres, not on the roadshow itinerary, holding individual film days.

Apart from film seasons, exhibitions, discussions, posters, T-shirts, stickers and a commemorative issue of British Film Year stamps, there will be innumerable local and national competitions. The first of these, sponsored by the *Sunday Times*, was a screenplay contest with a promise, to the winner, that his or her script would be made into a film produced by David Puttnam. It is, I believe, highly significant and a good omen for British Film Year that this competition, expected by the organisers to result in some six hundred entries, actually attracted four times as many.

The interest, indeed fascination, with films and film-making in this country undoubtedly exists. Our job as an industry, in British Film Year, is to harness that fascination to its proper focal point: the cinema.

Traditionally, it is the young who account for the largest proportion of admissions. Currently, 52 per cent of an average cinema audience is aged between 15 and 24. I do not believe that these young people go to the cinema just to romance in the back row or escape from parental supervision in the home. Indeed, when asked, they rated dancing far higher as a social activity for dating.

I believe that they go to the cinema for reasons that all of us went to the cinema – once. Because that is where you see the latest, the most newsworthy, the film that has generated the most excitement, the most want-to-see.

Another of the aims of British Film Year is to ensure that youngsters are introduced to cinema as part of the fabric of their lives. With this in mind, we have established a nationwide schools programme, aiming to place current releases on primary and secondary education curricula, reaching 11 million children. As well as study guides relating to particular films, we are making available, free of charge, teachers' documents which explore the links between film and drama, music, history and politics. The result will be that both pupils and teachers will go to cinemas as a normal extension of their regular classroom activities.

A decade ago this would have been impossible, unthinkable. It was then that film-making in general touched a nadir of exploitation, sex and violence. This was not, of course, limited to British films. But our indigenous industry, starting in the mid-Fifties, had also sacrificed what emerges today as its greatest strength: its own identity. We abandoned that birthright by a process of stultifying compromise, in ever-increasing and ultimately self-defeating attempts to pander to what we believed were the tastes of a world market.

We could not, it seemed, break free from a vicious circle. Greatly due to the then fresh impact of television, audiences diminished catastrophically. With attendances down, admission prices started to rise. In consequence attendances dropped still further, frequently to a point where cinemas were no longer commercially viable. Their prime siting in shopping centres meant that their sales value increased temptingly by leaps and bounds. There followed the process of 'rationalisation' whereby the sites were sold, and theatres that formerly housed one screen were divided to accommodate two or even three. Less staff meant more vandalism, and its ravages in a declining situation were too expensive to repair. Lack of repair and refurbishment led to audiences staying away in droves. With attendances a mere fraction of what was needed for a film to recoup its costs in this country alone, came the desperate and heartbreaking attempts to generate revenue from overseas. Particularly, of course, from the United States.

Successive governments acted too late or at the wrong time or did nothing at all to stem the tide. With minimal encourgement or incentive from Parliament, in spite of the fact that our technicians, artists, writers and directors are, and always have been, the envy of the world, the downward spiral inevitably continued. The failure, the inability of British films – with a few brilliant exceptions – to make a profit abroad frightened away potential investors. Those that did invest tended naturally to favour the proven formula, the sequel to an established success. And this, by definition, eradicated innovation, genuine creativity, and the vital emergence of new talent.

What kept the British film industry alive was very largely the skills of our technicians and the excellence of our facilities – allied to the weakness of Sterling, which meant that it was cheaper to make films here than in America. It was these factors which brought to our studios *Star Wars, Superman* and *Raiders of the Lost Ark*.

Then, in 1982, the tide began to turn. With the success of *Chariots of Fire,* both here and in the United States, came the rediscovery that the more indigenous our films, the greater their chance of real international appeal. When we proclaim our own views – be they of our society as it is today or of our past links with countries such as India – when our humour is British humour, then we are on firm ground.

At the four most recent American Awards ceremonies – followed, it is estimated, by one billion television viewers around the world – British films have been accorded an amazing total of seventeen Oscars. This is more than we had been awarded in the entire span of the previous fourteen years since *Oliver* swept the board in 1968. Whilst heartening for individual and national pride, Oscars are not, of course, in themselves a sign of revival in British cinema. But what they have meant, first with *Chariots* and then, a year later in 1983 with *Gandhi,* is that British films are able to earn vast sums of money in America and be placed in the league table of the highest grossing pictures ever made.

If we can woo, cajole and persuade just 4 per cent more people into our cinemas during 1985, the financial return to those who exhibit and distribute movies, and therefore to those who make them, becomes viable. With just that small degree of upturn we will be able to continue to venture, in both talent and subject matter, and make films that stand a chance of recouping their costs. The secret is that they should be truly our own, such as those creating a stir, as I write, at the very commencement of British Film Year. Productions like *The Shooting Party, A Private Function, Wetherby, Dance With A Stranger,* and *The Killing Fields.*

Perhaps film-making in Britain has finally come of age. Harnessed to techniques, skills and facilities which have always been without equal, new talent with contemporary ideas and fresh perspectives is finding a voice and a platform. We have found the means and the courage to be original, innovative and even eccentric. To be British, in fact. To succeed by being ourselves.

RICHARD ATTENBOROUGH
April 1985

Gilbert Adair revisits eight decades of British film-making from its modest but enterprising origins to the unmistakable promise of an artistic and commercial revival.

THE BRITISH TRADITION

PART ONE   by GILBERT ADAIR

PART ONE:
THE BRITISH TRADITION
by Gilbert Adair

'I've just seen Burt Lancaster in my viewfinder. Now I *know* I'm in the movie business.' That was Bill Forsyth speaking, in a humorous and revealing aside, to his producer, David Puttnam, while filming *Local Hero* on location in Houston, Texas. Presumably the making of its predecessor, *Gregory's Girl*, had also entailed the need for a camera and sound equipment and a shooting script; but, because Forsyth could see merely Gordon John Sinclair, the Gregory of the title, in his viewfinder, *he had not believed he was in the movie business.*

The anecdote is a slight one, and should not be invited to bear too much generalising weight. Yet, if Forsyth's ingenuous comment very likely referred to his own economically pinched early work, it does carry a wider application. Simplifying a bit, the history of the British cinema is that of an inferiority complex. When, in 1915, Hollywood graduated into its first pair of long trousers, D. W. Griffith's *The*

Birth of a Nation, the home grown product was still in rompers; artistically speaking, and, ever since, American movies have seemed oversized, over-budgeted, over-sexed and perennially over here. Then, just when the industry was beginning to feel more secure, in the immediate wake of the Second World War – with attendances peaking at an unheard-of and unsurpassed 1635 millions in 1946 – it was confronted by yet another, domestic 'major studio': the BBC. It was the BBC that unified the British people (doubly so with the advent of television), that permitted them to share, celebrate and nightly reaffirm a sense of national identity without un-Britishly having to quit the cosy security of their homes. And the Coronation of Elizabeth II in the summer of 1953 – a decisive boost to the sale of TV sets – was equally that of the new medium.

This inferiority complex also informs the way a fair proportion of British films have been conceived

THE BRIGHTON SCHOOL

The turn of the century saw the foundation of a number of small film companies invariably dominated by one man, who would write, produce, direct (even if the separate functions of producer and director were still to be defined) and perform in his own films. The most celebrated of these 'schools', as they were dubbed by the French historian Georges Sadoul, was located in Brighton, no doubt because the magic-lantern tradition out of which early filmic practices in Britain arose naturally gravitated towards a seaside resort.

The 'Brighton School' grouped, primarily, such pioneering figures as George Albert Smith, a former portrait photographer who developed the intercut close-up to focus on a group detail and the use of double exposure in trick photography; Esme Collings (a former partner of William Friese-Greene), who shot the first film, *The Broken Melody* (1896), in which a well-known stage actor, Auguste Van Biene (supported by his repertory company), made an appearance; and, most famously, James Williamson (1855-1933).

Williamson, who owned a chemist's and photographic shop in Hove in which he would develop, print and enlarge customers' snapshots, acquired a projector which he contrived to transform into a motion picture camera with the assistance of the engineer Alfred Darling. Using the garden of his own cottage for 'location shooting' and members of his own family as his *dramatis personae*, he made a series of popular one-reelers, including such titles as *Dear Boys Home For The Holidays* (1904), *Flying the Foam and Some Fancy Diving* (*circa* 1906) and *Two Little Waifs* (1907). He later turned his attention to the manufacture of cinematographic equipment and, by 1909, had wholly retired from film production.

The principal fascination of these pioneers resides (a) in their invention of novel cinematographic techniques (sometimes far in advance of other film-producing countries); (b) the documentary record of rural life of eight decades ago which they have left us; and (c) the evolution of dramatic, if mostly 'comic', narrative conventions: as befits their resort setting, many of Williamson's short comedies resembled nothing so much as moving seaside postcards.

However, with its increasing elaboration, sophistication and commercialisation, the cinema was soon to become a specialised, and indeed more compartmentalised, medium; and those early producers with a somewhat Jack-of-all-trades approach swiftly faded from prominence.

(Left) Alma Taylor and Chrissie White in an episode of Cecil Hepworth's popular *Tilly* series.

and perceived over the years. As far as their conception is involved, there are several obvious examples: the didactic bullishness of the documentary movement, the 'little England' whimsy of the Ealing comedy, even the winsomely larky fruits of the self-styled 'Swinging Sixties', when the emperor's new clothes could be purchased off the peg at Bibā and Mary Quant. As for the question of their critical (and public) 'image', the unfortunate truth is that, when not circumscribed by the jingoist swagger of the tabloid press, British film criticism of its own national cinema has tended to be narrowly sociological in tone.

The problem here is twofold. In the first place, it is almost the essence of the sociological approach that every work of art be treated as though it were by Anon, as though the artist himself were irrelevant. Its advocates, in consequence, risk straying into grey areas of judgment, where a more genuine critical perspective might have served to apply the brakes to some of their wilder assessments.

In the second place, 'reality' is, or ought to be, the filmmaker's *palette*, not his canvas. It is for him to mix the colours of that 'reality', before smearing the screen with them; for the critic to respond to the completed work, instead of worrying about the palette's gaudy, multi-hued dishevelment. And though it would be foolish to reduce the artistic impulse behind every film to its director's contribution only, even so one works on the assumption that, at the very least, a film 'takes after' its director, as a child is said to take after its parents.

All of which is by way of preface to the brief history of the British cinema that follows. It will, essentially, be a history of *achievement;* and, considering the richness of material, something of a sprint, something not unlike the surreal episode in Jean-Luc Godard's *Bande à part* when its trio of raffish protagonists scurry through the salons and corridors of the Louvre in an endeavour to break the speed record for viewing (or squinting at) the assembled treasures. (For any reader seeking a fuller acquaintance with the industry's evolution – political, economic, ideological – I recommend Roy Armes' *A Critical History of the British Cinema, British Cinema History*, edited by James Curran and Vincent Porter, and *Cinema and State* by Margaret Dickinson and Sarah Street.)

It would be an uphill task attempting to squeeze the various and complicated origins of the British cinema into a couple of tight paragraphs. A dutiful checklist of the best-known, if by now mostly forgotten, figures from the turn of the century, such as Cecil Hepworth, Will Barker, Walter Haggar, Birt

STARS OF THE SILENTS

Even in Britain, the origin of the star-system virtually coincided with that of the film industry itself. As in the United States, it was essentially from a theatrical background that these first stars were inducted, and film repertory companies were soon formed by the various British studios. An actor like Ronald Colman could casually assure his interviewer, 'I have said that I have seven million fans. In print that looks a bit boastful, but any star can count on having that number of people see his pictures.' If Colman's fame has proved more durable that that of most actors and actresses from the British silents, it is doubtless due to his early departure for Hollywood. Yet, though now largely forgotten, British film stars from the century's teens and twenties were hardly less idolised than their American counterparts.

Between 1910 and 1916, for instance, Fred Evans made a national reputation for himself as 'Pimple' in a long-running series of one-reel farces, mostly burlesques of the period's more prestigious productions. Evans was invariably decked out in an undersized cricket blazer and cap, baggy trousers and a thick, snaky muffler around his neck; and his technique never strayed far from the crude slapstick traditions of the circus. Comedy of a more sentimental – and, for the period, more authentically cinematic – type was purveyed by Alma Taylor, better-known of the two tomboy heroines of Cecil Hepworth's *Tilly* series. She topped a 1915 poll of popular stars (in which Charlie Chaplin, about to be signed up by Hollywood, was placed third) and

had still retained that position nine years later. An actress of exceptional delicacy and restraint – especially in two 1916 melodramas with Stewart Rome, *Annie Lawrie* and *Coming Thro' the Rye* – she was said never to have used make-up on the screen. Hepworth, the director with whom she was most closely associated but who declined ever to pay her more than sixty pounds a week, remarked that, when she was called upon to cry in a film, her tears were genuine. Though Taylor made a couple of forgotten talkies, and even acted in one of the very first live television plays, her career properly ended with that of the silent cinema. She died in 1974.

His qualities as a screen actor apart, Taylor's leading man, Stewart Rome, deserves a film history footnote to himself by having clearly defined the parameters of the star-system during the industry's pioneering years. In 1919 Cecil Hepworth sought to restrain him from calling himself 'Stewart Rome' in employments other than those which he, Hepworth, controlled. By winning the subsequent legal action, Rome established that an actor's professional name belonged to him rather than to the company which coined it for him. (Rome was, in fact, born Septimus Ryott.)

By the twenties, the British cinema could boast a fairly impressive roster of household names, a handful of which can still be conjured with today: the airily dapper musical comedy star Jack Buchanan; the wistfully handsome Leslie Howard, later to achieve international fame in Hollywood; the theatrical actor and author of *Dr. Syn*, Russell Thorndike, brother of the more famous Sybil; and that embodiment of English moral rectitude, Clive Brook, again destined for the American sound cinema. Of those who continued working on this side of the Atlantic, and almost inevitably saw their careers curtailed by the advent of sound, perhaps the most delightful was the roguishly pretty, golden-curled ingenue Betty Balfour, who could fairly be described as the British Clara Bow.

(Right) Alma Taylor, the British cinema's 'Eve' to Stewart Rome's 'Adam'.

'Street scenes, breaking waves, railway trains – anything that moved was grist to the mills we ground in those days.'
CECIL HEPWORTH

Like the recreations which they supplanted, the first British films were basically unauthored artefacts, naive, anecdotal and already derivative. Armes catalogues a number of plot synopses all lackadaisically cribbed from the medium's earliest work of fiction, *L'Arroseur arrosé*, which was shot, on their own garden lawn, by the Lumière brothers in the late 1890s: 'Boy treads on gardener's hose, then releases the water', 'Youth grips gardener's hose, then releases water', 'Boy tricks gardener by stepping on his hose, then releasing water', and so forth. While imbued with the mystery which most 'first things' would appear to possess (the mystery of the Lascaux cave drawings, for instance), and priceless to the film historian as documents, they cannot be said to deserve any close non-specialised attention.

With the century barely into its teens, modes of production, distribution and exhibition were established which bear an uncanny resemblance to those in force today. According to a survey by the 1914 edition of the *Kinematograph Year Book*, the country boasted 1167 picture houses, more than half of these within the Greater London area. The British Board of Film Censors was set up in 1912. Film studios were constructed not only in such expected locations as Ealing and Elstree and Teddington, but in Clapham, Victoria and St Albans as well. There existed so-called 'schools': the Brighton School, with James Williamson as presiding genius, was the most prestigious in its day. Cecil Hepworth's long-running *Tilly* cycle of comedies made household names, the British cinema's first, out of Alma Taylor and Chrissie White; and another series, *Winky*, featuring the comic Reggie Switz, ran up a total of 39 instalments. Finally, enterprising producers had already started to ransack the 1001 Tales of Shakespearazade with an eye to filmic adaptation. In 1913 Sir Johnston Forbes-Robertson, the theatrical knight, dazzled audiences with a mute and severely abridged *Hamlet*, a *Hamlet* with not much to offer *except* the Prince.

It was not until the mid-twenties, however, that a handful of still conjurable names contrived to stand out from the fog. These were, supremely, Alfred Hitchcock, also Anthony Asquith (known as 'Puffin'

Acres and R. W. Paul, would cause them to plop onto the page like so many name droppings. Who, after all, has actually seen Hepworth's *Rescued by Rover* (1905)? Or Haggar's *The Salmon Poachers*, made the same year?

The whole period has been covered expertly by Roy Armes in his *Critical History*. Armes is especially rewarding on how, in its infancy, the chameleonic medium assimilated the narrative codes and devices of then current forms of popular entertainment. Quoting from John L. Fell's *Film and the Narrative Tradition*, he submits that 'in the motion pictures there surfaced an entire tradition of narrative technique which had been developing unsystematically for a hundred years. It appears sporadically not only among the entertainments so far mentioned [which is to say, "the nineteenth-century novel, early comics, magazine illustration, the Cubists and Impressionists, the most pop of popular literature, and entertainments of the theatre, fairground and parlour"], but in ephemera as diverse as stereograph sets, peep shows, song slides, and postal cards.'

and son of the Liberal Prime Minister, Herbert Asquith), Herbert Wilcox, Adrian Brunel, Victor Saville, Walter Forde and Maurice Elvey, most prolific of British film-makers; the producer Michael (later Sir Michael) Balcon and the matinee idol Ivor Novello.

Hitchcock's is a case apart, and best left for last. Balcon's career extended right into the sixties, and his name is primarily associated with the Ealing comedies and dramas he supervised in the two decades previous to that. Asquith's involvement in filmmaking, too, would last almost until his death in 1968, but since neither his aims nor his methods changed in over forty years, he can usefully be dealt with here.

By all accounts, 'Puffin' Asquith was a delightful chap, urbane yet very friendly, something of a Bohemian dandy on the set, with his exquisitely cut dungarees and his viewfinder dangling onto his stringy pullover as nonchalantly as a monocle. In 1925, along with Bernard Shaw, H. G. Wells, the biologist Julian Huxley and others, he founded the Film Society, a milestone in the history of British film appreciation. As a director, however, his reputation is a good deal less secure. If the odd visual conceit in two early features – *A Cottage on Dartmoor* (1929) and *Tell England* (1931), a sentimental celebration of public school values tested in the crucible of Gallipoli – seemed to announce an aesthete's fidgety impatience with lower-middlebrow, semi-literary cinema, the subsequent ones soon quashed most such expectations. Where other directors would make movies consciously angled at the international film festival circuit, Asquith aspired no higher than the Royal Command Performance.

He adapted Shaw three times and Terence Rattigan four times. For those who admired him, he was a 'stylish' film-maker, which tends to mean, as it did in his case, upper-class. Even the best of his work – *Pygmalion* (co-directed in 1938 by its Higgins, Leslie Howard, and now most fondly remembered for Wendy Hiller's superb Eliza Dolittle) and *The Importance of Being Earnest* (1952, ditto for Edith Evans' Lady Bracknell) – looked like nothing so much as animated *Punch* cartoons, of a type published by George du Maurier *circa* 1905.

Herbert Wilcox's titles are so eloquent in themselves that critical commentary becomes all but redundant. Just consider, for starters, *The Little Damozel*, *London Melody*, *I Live in Grosvenor Square*, *The Courtneys of Curzon Street*, *Spring in Park Lane*, *Maytime in Mayfair*, *Lilics in the Spring* and *King's Rhapsody*. His 'patch', as one will observe, was encompassed by the three or four square miles of central London owned by the Duke of Westminster, whose posh streets with their creamy Georgian façades he remained in awe of for the rest of his life. His ambition, you might say, was to turn Belgravia into what it has always rather sounded like – a twee fairy-tale grand duchy, both English and Ruritanian. His best-known films, a pair of tributes to Queen Victoria, *Victoria the Great* and *Sixty Glorious Years*, starred his discovery Anna Neagle, whose own Prince Consort he was to become in 1934.

(Previous page left) An early poster for Reggie Switz's *Winky* comedies, whose capitalised claim ALL BRITISH pre-echoes Colin Welland's 'The British are coming!' of seventy years later. (Previous page right) So protracted was Queen Victoria's reign, it required two Herbert Wilcox biopics to encompass it: Anna Neagle in *Victoria the Great* (1937). (Above) 'Do you know your slip is showing?' 'No – but you hum it and I'll play it.' Ivor Novello in *The Vortex* (1937).

In justice to Wilcox, however, it has to be added that the predominantly working-class audiences of the thirties relished his fantasies of wish fulfilment (even if, at the close of his career, he signally failed to keep pace with public taste: his swan song but one, *The Lady is a Square*, 1959, an abortive mismatching of dowagers and teenagers, was particularly ill-judged). And since the movies from which the most insights may be gleaned concerning a society's aspirations are those which prove phenomenally popular within it, not those which purport to dwell on one or other of the problematic issues besetting it, Wilcox's work will continue to fascinate the social historian.

As for Adrian Brunel and Victor Saville, the former directed two talked-about adaptations in 1928, *The Constant Nymph*, from Margaret Kennedy's wispy bestseller, and *The Vortex*, from Noël Coward's theatrical *succès de scandale*, both of them featuring Ivor Novello, he of the celebrated profile. (Such male 'profiles' were as current in the twenties and thirties as Alpine busts were to be in the fifties.) At which point Brunel was caught up on the treadmill of 'quota quickies', low-budget, low-quality duds churned out by British studios in order to meet the requirements of the 1927 Cinematograph Act, which stipulated that up to thirty percent of all motion pictures screened in the United Kingdom had to be home-produced.

Not that his early work had exactly made for compulsive entertainment. In his autobiography, *The Youngest Son,* the critic and film historian Ivor Montagu had this to say about *The Vortex:* "Noël Coward's plot: 'Mother, will you give up lovers if I give up drugs?' of necessity became 'Mummy, will you give up going to teas and dances if I give up cigarettes and Aspirins?' "

CENSORSHIP

'. . . film propaganda will be most effective when it is least recognizable as such. Only on a few rare prestige films, reassurance films and documentaries should the government's participation be announced. The influence brought to bear by the Ministry on the producers of feature films, and encouragement given to foreign distributors, must be kept secret. This is particularly true of any films which it is hoped to distribute in America and other neutral countries . . .'
Ministry of Information, *Programme for Film Propaganda* (1939)

Perhaps the essential fact which requires to be understood about the British system of film censorship, established with the BBFC (British Board of Film Censors) in 1912, is that, though the State may actively discourage the making of a film by withholding government facilities instrumental in its production, it has no power to suppress it. Its sole influence, at least in theory, has been exerted in the matter of granting or denying an 'advisory' certificate for the benefit of local authorities. Since such a certificate became virtually a precondition of exhibition, however, it has meant in effect that, no matter what a director might feel free to record on celluloid, his or her film cannot hope for a conventional circuit release without prior authorisation from the BBFC.

The Board's concern is naturally not with the 'quality' of a film, only with its suitability for public exhibition. And the grounds on which any film might be denied a certificate were laid out in nine principal categories: (1) Religious; (2) Political; (3) Military; (4) Administration of Justice; (5) Social; (6) Questions of Sex; (7) Crime; (8) Cruelty; and (9) Sound. Thus, in relation to (5), a film treatment of Walter Greenwood's *Love on the Dole*, already a highly successful novel and play, was in the thirties twice refused by the Board, which cited a total ban on the use of 'relations between capital and labour' as a film's 'principal theme'. Oddly enough, this stricture was relaxed during the war years, the Ministry of Information being then eager to awaken the population to such socio-political questions, thereby encouraging a greater alertness to the necessity of the nation's anti-Nazi struggle. Another rule to be relaxed following the outbreak of hostilities was that relating to 'representations of living persons'. In 1939 it was quietly announced: 'During wartime our rule against the representation of living persons does not extend to enemy aliens.'

Over the years, the British censorship system has lurched from crisis to crisis, from challenge to challenge; from Joseph Strick's adaptation of Joyce's *Ulysses*, refused a classification by the Board and left to the discretion of invidual local authorities, to Sam Peckinpah's *Straw Dogs*, released with a number of disfiguring cuts; from soft- and hard-core porn films, generally screened in cinema 'clubs' as a means of escaping the BBFC's jurisdiction, to so-called 'video nasties', still very much an issue under debate. Though there have been regular calls for the abolition of censorship altogether, it would appear impossible to muster sufficient public support in the face of such militant opponents of the move as Lord Longford, Mary Whitehouse and the Festival of Light.

IVOR NOVELLO

The personification of the matinée idol, with his theatrical good looks and languid lounge lizard assurance, Ivor Novello (born Ivor Davies in Cardiff) virtually dominated the English musical stage during the interwar years. Yet, like the strikingly similar figure of Noël Coward, he displayed his versatility in several different spheres. His sumptuously escapist West End musicals – *Glamorous Night*, *The Dancing Years*, *King's Rhapsody* – were long-running and often revived, and many of them were subsequently filmed. He was also the composer of one of the best-known English tunes of the century, the patriotic World War I song *Keep the Home Fires Burning*. Novello's primary contribution to the cinema, however, was as an actor, in which capacity he starred in a number of British, Hollywood and Continental films. His best-known role remains that of the mysterious, fog-swathed stranger in Hitchcock's *The Lodger* (1926), a role which he reprised for a less memorable remake in 1932. Another silent Hitchcock drama in which he was to be seen, *Downhill* (1927), was based on his own play; and, in the same year, he appeared in the film version of Noël Coward's theatrical shocker of drugs and gigolos, *The Vortex*, playing the role made famous by Coward himself on the stage. Novello found the talkies rather less sympathetic as a medium, and definitively retired from the screen following his appearance in *Autumn Crocus* (1934). He died in 1951 at the age of 58.

(Left) **Profile of Ivor Novello. (Below) Ralph Richardson, Edna Best and John Clements in the fictitious English county of** *South Riding*.

Saville was a more curious, and beyond doubt a more capable, figure. His films, though frequently impersonal and unadventurous, at least bore a glancing resemblance to Hollywood's *vin ordinaire* from the same period. The musical *Evergreen* (1934), whose eupeptic leading lady, Jessie Matthews, was the thirties' Julie Andrews, was kitschy and charming, and Saville himself retained a special fondness for *South Riding* (1938), a sedate Home Counties soap opera.

Forde and Elvey kept the pot bubbling agreeably enough – for, in the latter case, over forty years and three hundred films. Both of them rose from the ranks, so to speak, to become, as directors, 'non-commissioned officers', responsible between them for an amazing quantity of star vehicles. Elvey it was who guided Gracie Fields (*Sally in Our Alley*), Jack Hulbert and Cicely Courtneidge (*Under Your Hat*), Arthur Askey (*You Lucky People*), etc, etc. Forde oversaw Hulbert (*Jack's the Boy*, *Jack Ahoy*, *Bulldog Jack*) and Askey (*Charley's Big-Hearted Aunt*), as well as the Crazy Gang (the very funny *Gasbags*), Gordon Harker (*Inspector Hornleigh on Holiday* and *Inspector Hornleigh Goes to It*), the radio star Tommy Handley (*It's That Man Again*) and, with a budget more generous than he was accustomed to, Sid Field (*The Cardboard Cavalier*).

'Sometimes you find that a film is looked at solely for its content, without any regard to the style or manner in which the story is told. And, after all, that, basically, is the art of the cinema.'
ALFRED HITCHCOCK

And there was Hitchcock. Alfred Hitchcock was a chess master who played blindfold against himself. A detective-poet who solved puzzles he himself had set. A one-man conspiracy. He was a cultivator of the purple patch, or set-piece, which is what we really mean when we call him the 'Master of Suspense'. He made some of the finest British films ever – such entertainments of enduring bewitchment as *The Man Who Knew Too Much, The Thirty-Nine Steps, The Lady Vanishes, Rich and Strange, Number Seventeen* (his seventeenth directorial credit, as it happens) and *Young and Innocent* (most remarkable for its extraordinary overhead shot tracking the entire length of a ballroom of dancers before zeroing on in the twitching black-faced minstrel murderer like an Exocet missile) – he made all these marvellous films, then upped and left for Hollywood, where, as is now generally conceded, he would direct a number of superior ones.

Why so? The truth is that Hitchcock understood, at a time when none of his compatriots apparently did, that the cinema was an audiovisual, not a literary, medium. He was the first to make the camera *earn its keep*, not as a mere recording device but as an amazingly versatile instrument – in turn, scalpel and truncheon, keyhole and bay window. What is more, as the medium's supreme deviser of thrillers, he must have been sensitive to the peculiarly gory implications of certain cinematic terms – shooting, cutting, etc. Not surprisingly, then, he soon ran afoul of what has proved to be the bane of the British cinema in its hundred-year existence – its chronic gentility, its pervasively prissy conformism.

A Buddha in a Savile row suit: Alfred Hitchcock on the set of _Frenzy_.

This, briefly, can be attributed to a variety of factors: the mostly upper middle-class origins of its directors and writers; the fetters of a predominantly literary culture; the ingrained conservatism of the industry's financial structure and the inflexible hierarchy of industrial relations within film production; the near-monopoly of the distribution system; the tight policing of the Board of Censors in all matters political, religious, social and sexual; and, perhaps, if such an entity may be said to exist, the British national 'character'.

An illustration of how Hitchcock's more latent impulses were neutralised in England is offered by *Rich and Strange* (1932), a little-known work much admired by partisans of his pre-American period. Whatever claims can be made for it, unfortunately, *Rich and Strange* is neither rich nor strange, though it might have been had Hitch ever elected to remake it in Hollywood. Such as it is, we shall find an amiable and utterly conventional comedy-drama about a couple of suburbanites – he's something in the City and she's something in the kitchen – who unexpectedly inherit a small fortune and set off on a world cruise. *En route,* they fall in with an aristocratic vamp and an earnest khaki-clad colonel; they seriously envisage divorce; they are shanghaied in Singapore; they swear undying love for each other during a shipwreck; and they are eventually rescued by a Chinese junk. The film ends, as you might predict, with them returning to their cosy little semi-detached and just as testy and alienated from their lot as at the outset.

If this catalogue of plot twists appears pretty implausible, the same is true of Hitchcock's best American films (notably, *Vertigo, North by Northwest, Psycho, The Birds* and *Marnie*). But what makes his mature work so much more disturbing and resonant is the way in which his protagonists are profoundly transformed by their ordeal: as the critic Robin Wood remarked, "A character is cured of some weakness or obsession by indulging it and living through the consequences." Nothing, however, in the whole jerky sequence of events traced out by *Rich and Strange*, has the slightest effect on the central couple, on their relationship to each other or their environment. Even if the film's rather tacky fantasy props had been endowed with a capacity to influence their behavioral development, how could it be reconciled with characters whose chinless stereotyped Britishness defines them as by nature resistent to it? Our hero and heroine revert to the suburban rut from which they have been fleetingly permitted to emerge – and that, the film

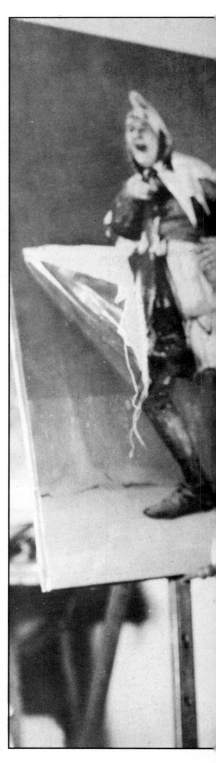

(Below) The Czech actress Anny Ondra in the very first British sound film, Hitchcock's *Blackmail* (1929). Since she proved incapable of enunciating comprehensive English, Hitch was forced to invent dubbing.

seems to be implying, is *where they belong*. It is clear that the narrative codes operating in the British cinema of the thirties were designed specifically to keep people in their place, be it social, emotional or sexual; and not even Hitchcock was able to do more than slavishly endorse them.

Thus the proposal which, in 1939, he received from David Selznick to direct his first Hollywood movie, *Rebecca*, represented not merely commercial

promotion but a timely opportunity to cut loose from a cinema whose dominant emotional register would be for some time to come, to quote one critic, "not so much one of desire frustrated as of the impossibility of desire". And, interestingly, one of his best British films was his last, *Frenzy*, dating from more 'permissive' 1972 and starring Jon Finch, Anna Massey, Barry Foster and Alec McCowen. The director made his familiar signatory appearance in the opening sequence, goggling at a corpse being dredged from the Thames and, in his outsize stockbroker's suit, looking like Gilbert and George rolled into one. His amused abhorrence of his native country – its food, its pubs, its police, the repressed sexuality of its inhabitants, which he externalised in the choosing of a cast of uniform physical uncomeliness – oozed from every pore of the screen, making it the most joyously bilious of all his films. It was, more significantly, saturated in desire, albeit of a homicidal bent; and it's worth nothing how briskly and brusquely it ended, with the arrest of the sex strangler played by Foster, but without the *status quo* being given time to re-assert itself.

The codes from which Hitchcock managed to escape only by departing for Hollywood ran through the British cinema, from top to bottom, from upmarket to down, like the word 'Brighton' through a stick of rock. Saville's *South Riding*, for instance, concluded with a Tory squire donating land to the local council for a workers' housing scheme; with a pair of speculators caught red-handed in real estate chicanery: with a token rebel recanting his socialist (meaning 'un-British') principles, and finally – on George VI's Coronation Day, no less – with gentry and lower orders celebrating the achieved consensus in a communal rendition of 'Land of Hope and Glory'. A popular Gracie Fields (and J. B. Priestley-scripted) comedy of 1934, *Sing As We Go*, similarly proposed that class tensions were best resolved by some spontaneous musical outpouring. Filmed at the Depression's height, and dealing with the mass closure of Lancashire cotton mills, its basic premise was that social harmony would prevail if everybody, employers and employees alike, upheld the faith. "If we can't weave, we can still sing," she chirrups perkily. Also "We'll be able to practise while we're all queuing up for the dole!" In fact, Gracie declines to swell the dole queue, preferring to whisk herself off to Blackpool, a traditional playground for the working classes of the North, until the mill is rescued from closure by a miraculously advanced technological process.

'I've always found something funny in the idea of a hopelessly inefficient man blundering through a job he knows nothing about.'

WILL HAY

Only unrepentant 'skivers', it appeared, were left to provide any resistance to the period's dominant ideology. Which is why the dishevelled figure of Will Hay remains such a lovably boozy oasis in the British cinema of the thirties – our very own, uncrabby W. C. Fields. Redolent of chalk dust, mothballs, whiskey on the breath, and whiffy breakfast kippers, he represents, alongside Fields and Chaplin, the personification of what has been, in a medium overly preoccupied with thugs, psychopaths and assorted agents of bodily violence, a sadly neglected comic type: the seedy or disreputable. No one need feel hesitant about applying the term 'classic' to the best of his films, the farce *Oh, Mr. Porter!*, directed by Marcel Varnel in 1937.

WILL HAY

'I'm not putting forward anything startlingly original when I say that comedy must always border on drama. A good comedy scene is very near pathos. The character I portray is really a very pathetic fellow. It would never do, of course, to let the public be conscious of this pathos on the screen. But it's there all the same. In the same way, people mustn't be conscious of the fact that you're trying to be funny. Once they get this impression, you're no longer funny – and once they feel that you're pathetic, you are even less funny.'

Will Hay's modest self-analysis offers an accurate description of his own considerable cinematic appeal. Born in Stockton-on-Tees in 1888, and for many years a popular music-hall and radio comedian, Hay became one of Britain's top box-office stars in the thirties and forties. So successful was he, in fact, that he was mimicked by Michael Redgrave in Hitch-cock's *The Lady Vanishes*, a gag which tends to mystify audiences of the film today. Hay's most familiar and beloved characterisation was of a nervily insecure and semi-educated drifter propelled by chance into a position of authority for which he is intellectually unfit. Thus he often played schoolmasters scarcely more informed than his unruly pupils (in *Boys Will Be Boys*, 1935, *The Goose Steps Out*, 1942, etc.); or else a policeman (*Ask a Policeman*, 1939), a lawyer (*My Learned Friend*, 1944) and, most famously, a station-master (*Oh, Mr. Porter!*, 1937). In the majority of his early comedies he was seconded by two droll character actors: Graham Moffatt, an ageless 'Fat Boy', and Moore Marriott, a wizened codger, both as sly and seedy as Hay himself. Subsequently, however, wishing to establish his own personality without their support and perhaps hoping to broaden his appeal, he dropped them from his films. Hay died in 1949.

S. 211

> 'I suppose in films the art – as Mr. Dulles said of diplomacy – is to come to the brink of bankruptcy and stare it in the face.'
> **ALEXANDER KORDA**

> 'You can't direct a Laughton picture. The best you can hope for is to referee.'
> **ALFRED HITCHCOCK**
> **on CHARLES LAUGHTON**

Even more than Hitchcock, perhaps, it was Alexander Korda who contrived (for a while) to dispel the British industry's pervasive sense of inferiority towards the Hollywood product. Korda was born near Budapest in 1893. By the time he was twenty-five, he had been responsible for two dozen features in his native country. Without ever easing up on his phenomenal output, he travelled into exile in Berlin and Vienna, briefly stopped over in Hollywood, then returned to Europe via France, where he adapted one of Marcel Pagnol's Marseilles trilogy, *Marius*, in 1931. He docked in England the same year with, in his generous wake, a clan of Hungarian relatives who must have been, collectively, as witty as a barrel of monkeys.

(Left) The inimitable (though much imitated) Will Hay as *Windbag the Sailor* (1936). (Below) A poster for the movie buff: Charles Laughton as Henry and Wendy Barrie as . . . which one of his wives, in Korda's *The Private Life of Henry VIII* (1933)?

Korda subscribed to the belief that moderation in everything was moderation *to excess;* and, carefully trimming his own natural flamboyance, he evolved a style which might be described as one of *excess in moderation.* His company, London Films (for which brand new studios were built at Denham), was as distinct from Ealing Films as London was distinct from Ealing, that middle-class, slightly down-at-the-heel suburb outlying the capital. And his vision was shaped by the tribal myths of his adopted country's Establishment class, as witness the genres with which we tend to associate his studio – historical melodramas, brittle drawing-room comedies and jingoistic yarns of the Raj and Empire.

Korda's best-known work was *The Private Life of Henry VIII,* which he directed in 1933 with Charles Laughton in the title role, Laughton's wife Elsa Lanchester as Anne of Cleves and a discovery of Korda's, Merle Oberon, as Anne Boleyn. Henry – his gargantuan appetites and his marital antics – was already one of the nation's most cherished folk myths, but this film, and in particular Laughton's performance, hands grimly on hips and legs akimbo, crystallised it. Since when, the stereotype has jelled into a hard gummy paste. No matter that historians or even those pop history partworks you notice pinned up in newspaper kiosks struggle to reverse the trend, pointing out that Henry was in reality a profoundly cultivated and enlightened monarch . . . not all that fat, either, and certainly no uncouth gourmandiser – no matter, Henry VIII is once and for all time as Laughton portrayed him. As for the film, it was an extremely lively specimen of history as viewed from the servants' quarters: no masterpiece, to be sure, but it thoroughly merited its success on both sides of the Atlantic.

Korda attempted an encore in 1934 with *The Private Life of Don Juan,* starring Douglas Fairbanks Sr. The situation, of an ageing Don by now incapable of sustaining repeated assaults upon the myth of his virility, was not startlingly original, and it made for a film as languid as its protagonist. By contrast, *Rembrandt* (1936), with Laughton again and some lifelike Dutch interiors exquisitely lit by Georges Périnal, was an affecting account of the painter's spiritual decline following the death of his wife. Korda's three remaining films as a director – *Lady Hamilton* (1941), a costume romp with Laurence Olivier and Vivian Leigh, *Perfect Strangers* (1945), an undistinguished romantic comedy, and *An Ideal Husband* (1947) – were without interest, and it was principally as an autocratic studio boss, a proponent of what might be called the 'Tsar-system'

(Right) A full-frontal George Formby.

Dean, however, he became, astonishingly, the country's top male performer at the box-office. 'Ah know nuthin aboot filming but ah'll have a bash. It's the thing to get in these days, isn't it?' Formby, true to the gormless character he portrayed, is reported to have replied when offered his first film role. Yet he proved regularly jealous of his co-stars (notably running afoul of Florence Desmond, the impersonator, during the filming of *No Limit*) and con-

temptuous of his directors. Formby's best-known comedies, now occasionally on television, were *Keep Fit* (1937), *Trouble Brewing* (1939), *Let George Do It* (1940) and *Turned Out Nice Again* (1941), its title being one of his catch-phrases). He died, following a belated return to the stage, in 1961.

The more bracing figure of Gracie Fields, good-humoured and warm-hearted, also managed to appeal to Southerners; and even to Amer-

icans after her much-criticised departure for Hollywood in 1940. (Her husband, Monty Banks, an Italian-born film producer, would almost certainly have been interned in England; and, it was later revealed, Churchill personally encouraged the couple to leave.) 'Our Gracie' was a genuine working-class icon, the best of whose films – *Sally in Our Alley* (1931), *Looking on the Bright Side* (1932), *Love, Life and Laughter* (1933) and *Sing As We Go*

(1934) – can still be appreciated as cheerful populist entertainments.

Other figures from the music-hall world to have enjoyed public, if rarely critical, success in the cinema were the Crazy Gang, 'Old Mother Riley' and Kitty McShane (the former played in drag by Arthur Lucan), and the 'Cheekie Chappie' Max Miller, whose suggestive material had to be considerably emasculated for national release.

of film production, that he continued to wield influence.

Because he employed prestigious collaborators in almost every department, especially those which controlled the 'look' of a film – sets, costumes and cinematography – Korda's most characteristic productions were plush Edwardian entertainments. Some of these can still provide real pleasure (*Knight Without Armour*, starring a languorous Marlene Dietrich, *Storm in a Teacup*, *The Scarlet Pimpernel*); some of them have aged rather badly (*The Rise of Catherine the Great*, *Sanders of the River*, *The Drum*); and all of them complacently conform to the heresy that the only stories worth telling are those involving Top People (as they used to say in ads for *The Times*).

On occasion he hired major film-makers from outside Britain: René Clair for *The Ghost Goes West* (1935), about a kilted wraith wafted across the Atlantic when his castle is purchased by an American tycoon; Robert Flaherty for the semi-documentary *Elephant Boy* (1937); and Josef von Sternberg for the uncompleted *I Claudius* (also 1937), which, from the evidence of fragments disclosed in *The Epic That Never Was*, BBC television's documentary on the affair, might have been the most extraordinary film ever shot in this country. His were, however, essentially a producer's films, with the curious soullessness that results from the absence of a director's Cyclops eye.

(Right) The artificial eye: Michael Powell. (Top left) Alexander Korda on the set of *The Scarlet Pimpernel*. (Bottom left) Leslie Howard and Merle Oberon contemplate the latter's portrait in *The Scarlet Pimpernel* (1935).

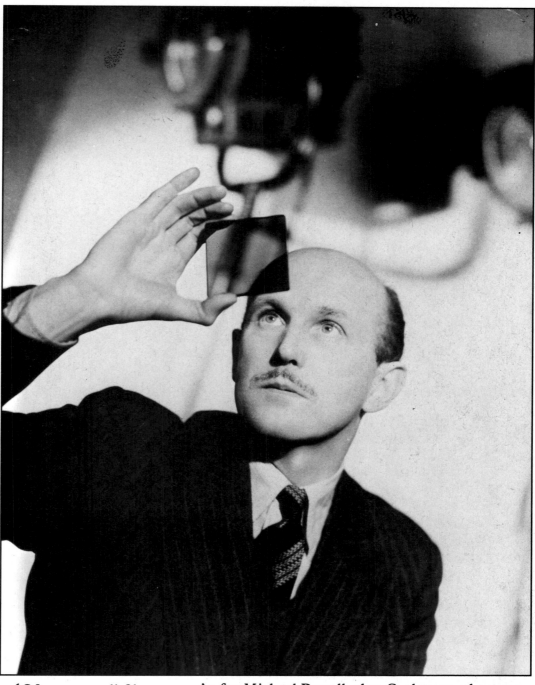

'Of course, all films are surrealist. They are because they are making something that looks like a real world but isn't.'
MICHAEL POWELL

As for Michael Powell, that Cyclops eye became a motif of his work, beginning with an arrow piercing a bullseye, the trademark of The Archers, a production company which he co-founded with his collaborator and screenwriter Emeric Pressburger in the forties.

In recent years, Powell has so often been written about as a neglected director that he is fast turning into one of the most exhaustively documented of all film-makers. Yet, he is, in the context of the British cinema's penchant for genteel 'realism', a genuine test case, which is why his career deserves to be examined in some detail.

Consider, for instance, what has to be the most idiosyncratic of even his films, *A Canterbury Tale*, made in 1944. For so long has this brainchild of his been labelled 'the one about the man who pours glue on girls' heads in the blackout' that one is liable to come to it unprepared for its thematic richness. That mysterious glue is merely the stuff which holds it all together.

It concerns a trio of twentieth century 'pilgrims' – an American GI, an English officer and a land girl (a wartime agricultural labourer) – travelling towards Canterbury, the Anglican Church's 'holy city', and meanwhile making the serendipitous discovery that everything is connected: past and present (the land girl seems to hear lingering echoes of mediaeval revelry, echoes which are also 'picked up' by the soundtrack); England and America (the GI swaps tree lore with a local timber merchant); high and low culture (the officer, a cinema organist in civilian life, is invited to play in Canterbury Cathedral).

In this, the role of the Glue Man himself (a magistrate disheartened by the fact that the local soldiery prefer spending their evenings off in feminine company to attending his illustrated lectures on the region's history!) is a dottily peripheral one. He *is* sigificant, however, as a symptom of the innate sense of decorum which acts as a curb on Powell's bravura assaults upon the canons of good taste. Thus it never strikes the amateur sleuths that there might be some dark sexual gratification lurking behind this uniquely peculiar mode of retribution – that, whatever the reason might be, pouring glue on girls' heads is *sick*. The question goes unraised, except in the spectator's mind. For a director famed for his kinkiness, Powell never quite succeeds in shaking off a very British sense of the proprieties. A case in point is *Black Narcissus* (1947), based on a Rumer Godden novel about a squad of near-hysterical nuns

(Top left) An exquisitely lit still from Michael Powell and Emeric Pressburger's *A Canterbury Tale*. (Top right) The designer Alfred Junge, director Michael Powell and screenwriter Emeric Pressburger inside Canterbury Cathedral for the shooting of *A Canterbury Tale* (1944). (Right) *Black Narcissus* 1947.

(Left) The greatest British film? Karl Boehm in Michael Powell's *Peeping Tom* (1960). (Right) Anton Walbrook turns up the three of spades in Thorold Dickinson's *The Queen of Spades* (1949).

cloistered in the Himalayas. Somewhat to one's disappointment, the object of its much fabled eroticism turns out to be David Farrar's knees, of all unlikely things; as the Maharajah's agent, he suggestively lolls around the virginal dovecot in khaki shorts.

Where Powell did excel was in belying Truffaut's famous claim of a fundamental incompatibility between England, as visual raw material, and the cinema. Half-Tory, half-dreamer, he could hardly have been better equipped for the task. By transforming cartoonist David Low's pompous, blinkered archetype into a choleric though lovable old codger, he made *The Life and Death of Colonel Blimp* (1943) almost an elegy for the English military caste, muddling through to eventual victory. With Roger Livesey giving the performance of a lifetime, Blimp's dogged progress through some superbly designed settings – London clubland, the War Office, a country estate, a Turkish bath, a bunkered wireless studio situated, as it were, 20,000 leagues under the BBC – had all of the magical whimsicality of a Stanley Spencer fresco. Winston Churchill tried to have the film suppressed, just as Blimp himself would probably have done.

Commissioned in 1946 to make a propaganda film that might contribute to easing the then strained Anglo-American alliance, Powell devised *A Matter of Life and Death*, in which a pilot (David Niven) plummets headlong from his blazing aircraft and, despite being already booked into the hereafter, survives. Whereupon a passionate debate as to his ultimate destiny – and, by a none too obvious extension, that of the two squabbling nations – rages in a monochrome Heaven, the film commuting wittily between colour and black-and-white. For

sheer impudence of invention, his wartime thrillers, *Contraband* (1940) and *One of Our Aircraft is Missing* (1942), can stand comparison with British Hitchcock. And a taut little *film noir* about a half-demented bomb disposal expert, *The Small Back Room* (1948), proves that he could well dispense with elaborate sets and colour consultants if need be. Only the musical extravaganzas, with the exception of *The Red Shoes* (1949), seem to me unworthy of their (and his) reputation.

Powell's most admired, maybe most personal, work is *Peeping Tom*, shot in 1959 from a screenplay by Leo Marks. Let Roy Armes summarise its plot. 'It is basically the story of a young man Mark (Karl Boehm) whose life has been crippled by his having been used as a guinea pig in his father's medical and scientific experiments in terror while still a child. Totally withdrawn and isolated from the world, Mark is fascinated by watching fear on the faces of others. An added complexity derives from the fact that Mark is a photographer whose obsession drives him to film in 16mm the death throes of a series of female victims. His camera incorporates both a lethal stake and a mirror directed back at the model, so that all the victims (women who as whore, pin-up or starlet are accustomed to being looked at) are now filmed by Mark as they are forced to watch their own death throes.'

Though critics of the day were aghast at its violence and sexual candour, I doubt that anyone would now dispute the 'sincerity' of *Peeping Tom* as an exploration of filmic voyeurism, a confirmation of film as an implicitly pornographic medium and of the screen as perhaps elaborate wall graffiti. The British cinema had never known anything quite like

it. Yet, if Powell was indeed exorcising his intimate demons, he could apparently do so only by imposing upon his material an intricate grid of eccentric 'personal touches'. The film abounds in private jokes (Powell himself plays the sadistic father while his own son plays Mark as a child; the name 'Mark Lewis' is an inversion of 'Leo Marks') and shriekingly loud Expressionistic visuals. Now take another look at Armes' synopsis. Remind you of anyone? Of course, Hitchcock's father did not exactly terrorise him with pseudo-scientific experimentation. Yet there was that anecdote, a much-publicised one, about chubby little Alf being incarcerated in a police station cell for about ten minutes. Nor could it be claimed for Hitchcock that he was 'totally withdrawn and isolated from the world'. Yet his last years, as we know, were increasingly lonely ones. As for such clinical phrases as '. . . whose obsession drives him to film the death throes of a series of female victims . . .', '. . . fascinated by watching fear on the faces of others . . .' and (more figuratively) '. . . his camera incorporates both a lethal spike and a mirror directed back at the model . . .', it is certainly possible to read them as a resumé of Hitchcock's own strategies as a director.

I do not intend to imply that Hitchcock, like the protagonist of *Peeping Tom*, could be described, even potentially, as any kind of homicidal psychopath. As a film-maker, however, he himself was a Peeping Tom, a voyeur, and he transformed the spectator into one as well. He lived out his obsessions *through* film where Powell could only record his *on* film. In *Vertigo*, for instance, Hitchcock not only made a brief cameo appearance, he unashamedly exposed himself in every frame of the film, as though his psyche were being strip-searched. Powell, on the other hand, straitjacketed by his Britishness, found himself becoming more and more artsy-fartsy; and the decline in his work would culminate in such truly baffling aberrations as *Honeymoon* (1958), *The Queen's Guards* (1961) and *They're a Weird Mob* (1966).

Much the same fate befell Thorold Dickinson, a maverick whose fastidious career got under way, like Powell's, in quota quickies of the thirties. Dickinson directed only eight features, of which *Gaslight* (1940, from Patrick Hamilton's literally creaky shocker), *The Queen of Spades* (1949, from a novella by Pushkin), and *Secret People* (1952) were the most notable. Even if currently forgotten, these films were dynamically edited, fluid and sharply framed, and unusual (in a British context) for their use of deep-focus, high-contrast photography. In fact, they were models, textbooks for the aspiring young film-maker. Unfortunately, 'textbooks' is the word. Dickinson filmed *by the book*. For all their brilliantly finicky perfectionism, his films were marbly objects, stylish but staid – his was, in a way, perfectionism without perfection, a dispiriting artistic mode.

Each of these artists – Hitchcock, Powell and Dickinson – saw his sensibility inhibited by British decorum, understatement, fear of eroticism and a refusal to take film seriously. Each of them, as he was able, strove to overcome the odds stacked against him. In the end, however, Hitchcock left for Hollywood. Powell standardised his fitfully impudent unpredictability. As for Dickinson, he declined into silence, teaching and neglect.

'**The story of the documentary movement is, in part, the story of how, not without a scar or two, we got by.**'

JOHN GRIERSON

The G.P.O. documentarists, under the dual aegis of John Grierson and Alberto Cavalcanti, have not precisely been neglected. Even so, the substantial body of work produced by the movement between 1929 and the Second World War now seems more remote than Dickinson's. Grierson was a myopic, mildly pugnacious Scot with an unwavering faith in the educational and propagandist properties of his chosen medium. Though he was no Marxist, his aesthetic credo, in which the working classes would affirm their dignity through being systematically more *photogenic* than the bourgeoisie, shared a pool of ideological assumptions with socialist realism. The model was Sergei Eisenstein, the great Soviet film-maker, idolised by Grierson. But what he absorbed from Eisenstein were his worst, most crassly manipulative ideas, those from *Que Viva Mexico,* whose sculptural peons, gracefully silhouetted against some grandiose St. Sebastianish cacti, expire in a variety of sultry postures while their gringo oppressors flop dead how and where they can. That said, in *Drifters* (1929), the only film which Grierson directed and which centred on the voyage of a Scottish trawler, there were individual images almost worthy of Eisenstein; and, in the British cinema, it was a novel occurrence in itself actually to depict men at their jobs.

Grierson was the documentary movement's ideologue, and his catechism, cited in a published collection of his essays, is worth re-quoting in full:

'(1) We believe that the cinema's capacity for getting around, for observing and selecting from life itself, can be exploited in a new and vital art form. The studio films largely ignore this possibility of opening up the screen on the real world. They photograph acted stories against artificial backgrounds. Documentary would photograph the living scene and the living story.

'(2) We believe that the original (or native) actor, and the original (or native) scene, are better guides to a screen interpretation of the modern world. They give cinema a greater fund of material. They give it power over a million and one images. They give it power of interpretation over more complex and astonishing happenings in the real world than the studio mind can conjure up or the studio mechanism recreate.

(**Right**) *Song of Ceylon* (1934) directed by Harry Watt.

ALBERTO CAVALCANTI

Alberto Cavalcanti was responsible for the G.P.O.'s more whimsical strain, being one of the most consistently bizarre and versatile figures in world cinema. Brazilian-born, he first became involved in the medium as part of the Parisian avant-garde in the twenties. He subsequently directed a number of French features of his own, the best of which were works of an intense poetic realism (e.g. *Rien que les heures*, 1926, *En Rade*, 1927). Accepting Grierson's invitation in 1934 to join the G.P.O. Unit, he proceeded to make some arch-characteristic G.P.O. documentaries (e.g. *Pett and Pott*, 1934, *Coal Face*, 1935). In 1942 he joined up with Michael Balcon, turning out a cluster of no less characteristic Ealing films, the most memorable of which were *Champagne Charlie* (1944, with the music-hall comedian Tommy Trinder), *Nicholas Nickelby* (1947) and the spooky 'Ventriloquist's Dummy' episode of the compendium fantasy *Dead of Night* (1945). Following his stint at Ealing, he returned to Brazil, before globetrotting all over again, via Austria (where he adapted – to the dramatist's satisfaction – Brecht's *Herr Puntila und sein Knecht Matti*), Romania, Italy and Israel.

The most striking of Cavalcanti's British films was *Went the Day Well?* (1942), an eerily plausible Graham Greene tale of a placid Gloucestershire village on whose inhabitants it gradually dawns that the corps of Royal Engineers billeted on them are in reality disguised German paratroopers.

'(3) We believe that the materials and the stories thus taken from the raw can be finer (more real in the philosophic sense) than the acted article. Spontaneous gesture has a special value on the screen.'

This fine manifesto, unfortunately, was confounded by about eighty percent of the G.P.O.'s output. Consider *Song of Ceylon*, a documentary directed in 1934 by Harry Watt. To be sure, Watt firmly rejects all those gross 'acted stories' and 'artificial backgrounds' so typical of studio-shot films. But cinematic artifice may assume a number of shapes and disguises. What, for instance, if not artifice, is a score by the English neoclassical composer Walter Leigh; a modish 'sound collage' devised by Cavalcanti; a commentary based on a voyager's account of the island in 1680 *(1680!)*; and a gaudily romanticised vision of the Ceylonese as a dusky, childlike, God-fearing people, as cute and playful as squirrels?

If that description makes *Song of Ceylon* sound just a trifle patronising, it should be said that the G.P.O. was egalitarian to the last: it was the whole human race which it patronised. The barrel-thumbed craftsmen depicted in Flaherty's *Industrial Britain* (1933) emerged as locally based 'natives', earthy indigenes not unlike the Ceylonese, albeit dourer and, in physique, considerably less alluring. The most durable of the Unit's films were those which tended to disregard Grierson and his articles of faith, such as the abstract shorts of Len Lye (*Colour Box, Rainbow Dance, Trade Tattoo*); the impertinent squibs directed by, and often starring, Richard Massingham (*Tell Me If It Hurts, And So To Work, The Five-Inch Bather*); and a film like Basil Wright and Harry Watt's *Night Mail* (1936), which 'set' the London-Glasgow run of a mail train to the verse of Auden and the music of Britten.

Ultimately, the (noble) failure of the documentary movement can be traced to Grierson's well-intentioned paternalism. His notion of how to dignify the downtrodden masses – positioning them against dark, lowering skies or raising the camera higher and higher on a crane until its subjects seem so many cloth-capped dots stranded amid row after identical row of semi-detacheds (a device that always reminds me of the affectation of children, when corresponding with their pen pals, of expanding the formulary address of house number, street and city to take in *England, Great Britain, Europe, The Western Hemisphere, The World, The Solar System* and *The Universe*) – ended up by reflecting, as one commentator rightly observed, 'the ethos of the Establishment no less than the imperial epics of Alexander Korda'.

The influence of the Second World War on the British cinema was threefold. First, it promoted a new genre, 'the British war film', one which was to prove a mainstay of the industry, offering steady above- and below-decks employment to such as Jack Hawkins, John Mills, Richard Attenborough and Richard Todd for decades to come. Second, it shifted the documentary school from the margin to the mainstream. Third, it made possible the emergence of Humphrey Jennings, the greatest of British documentarists.

The war film was essentially a postwar phenomenon and will be dealt with in its place. As for the ascension of the documentary movement, what it signified was that the genre had found an issue commensurate with, and a social climate receptive

to, Grierson's high hopes for the medium (though his own star, curiously, started to wane after 1939, when the G.P.O. Unit, renamed the Crown Unit, was incorporated into the official war effort). The number of war films, fictional or non-fictional, made in Britain between 1939 and 1945 far surpassed that of the Continental nations, most of the latter being, admittedly, under occupation. These were films like Harry Watt's *London Can Take It* (1940) and *Target For Tonight* (1941); John Boulting's *Desert Victory* (1943), *Tunisian Victory* (1944, co-directed with Frank Capra) and *Burma Victory* (1945); Pat Jackson's Technicolor tribute to the merchant navy, *Western Approaches* (1944); and Carol Reed and Garson Kanin's *The True Glory* (1945). They were often as popular with audiences as the 'escapist' entertainments of the same period, and served their purpose admirably and even movingly, that purpose being to boost morale. In 1945, when their directors returned to civvy (i.e. Wardour) street, they found themselves, like more than one officer who had enjoyed 'a good war', unable to cast off warm, nostalgic recollections of the British cinema's Big Push.

'I perceive also the hues of the men who built the city
The quarrymen cutting the slate, the furnace men, men underground, men felling timber
Each a brain, a peculiar skill, a knot of passions, breathing being, living soul.'
HUMPHREY JENNINGS (*As I Look*)

(Left) *The True Glory* (1945) directed by Carol Reed and Garson Kanin. (Above) *Fires Were Started* (1943) directed by Humphrey Jennings.

Humphrey Jennings was quite a different case. To begin with, prior to his involvement in the cinema, he had already established himself as a literary scholar, set designer, painter and social historian, his work in the latter discipline culminating in the uncompleted and as yet unpublished *Pandemonium*, a prodigious anthology of texts relating to the Industrial Revolution. Though the G.P.O. Unit had variously employed Jennings on a few thirties shorts, Grierson distrusted, maybe even feared, the poetic eclecticism of his magpie sensibility; and it was not until the following decade that he directed a trio of minor but authentic masterpieces of world cinema – namely, *Listen to Britain* (1941), *Fires Were Started* (1943) and *A Diary For Timothy* (1945, with a commentary by E. M. Forster, who had been one of Jennings' professors at Cambridge).

ALEC GUINNESS

(Top left) Alec Guinness and Joan Greenwood in Robert Hamer's *Father Brown*. (Bottom left) *The Ladykillers*, with Peter Sellers. (Above) With director David Lean on *Bridge on the River Kwai*.

'I prefer full-length camera shots because the body can act better than the face.'

The figure who most prominently represented British cinema from the immediate postwar years to the early sixties was tall, thin, shy, physically unprepossessing and as unlike the received notion of an international film star as it would be possible to conceive. Alec (later Sir Alec) Guinness began his professional life as an advertising copywriter; then, after training at the Fay Compton Studio of Dramatic Art, he gained a reputation as a classical actor during several consecutive seasons at the Old Vic and made a remarkable film debut as Herbert Pocket in David Lean's *Great Expectations*. There followed his unforgettably oily and dishevelled Fagin in the same director's *Oliver Twist;* all eight murder victims in Robert Hamer's *Kind Hearts and Coronets;* and, especially the cycle of Ealing comedies for which he is perhaps most fondly remembered: *A Run For Your Money, The Lavender Hill Mob, The Man in the White Suit* and *The Ladykillers* (in which he slipped into a deliciously toothy and sinister impersonation of Alastair Sim). Guinness's subsequent, and more international, filmography has seemed less uniformly impressive, despite the Oscar awarded him for his bravura performance as a half-demented martinet in Lean's *The Bridge on the River Kwai*. In compensation, however, the percentage which he earned for his appearance in *Star Wars* has made him a multimillionaire.

Guinness was a character actor in an almost parodically literal sense, apparently donning each of his characterisations in turn as another man might change hats. Yet, especially in recent years, an ambiguously steely quality has infected the tight-lipped yet boyishly sunny smile with which one had become familiar from his Ealing comedies; and the more subtle and resonant of his performances have been achieved without the sometimes dubious benefit of wigs and elaborate make-up. When one considers how elusive and ill-defined his facial features have remained, the effect is all the more disquieting.

PETER SELLERS

(Above) *Dr. Strangelove or How I Learned to Stop Worrying and Love The Bomb.* (Top right) With Sophia Loren *The Millionairess.* (Bottom right) *Heavens Above.*

By an odd coincidence, the popularity of Alec Guinness as the British cinema's leading comic character actor was to be eclipsed by that of Peter Sellers, a performer of remarkably similar gifts. Even in minor roles Sellers made an instant impression. Or rather, innumerable impressions. For no actor in film history, not even Guinness, so eerily immersed himself in the characters he played, to the point were Sellers himself was plagued by crises of identity and a sense, when offscreen, of personal inadequacy. From his earliest performances one still recalls with astonishing clarity his gormless Teddy Boy in *The Ladykillers* (1955), his befuddled old projectionist in *The Smallest Show on Earth* (1957) and his droll Tom-and-Jerry double act with Terry-Thomas in *Tom Thumb* (1958).

Though initially reluctant to tackle the role, he offered the British cinema one of its greatest character studies as a pompous, hen-pecked shop steward in the Boulting Brothers' *I'm All Right, Jack* (1959); so uncanny was his metamorphosis, both physical and vocal, that the film's crew fell uneasily silent when he strolled onto the set. Rumours already circulated, however, concerning his monstrously egotistical behaviour. When this could be attributed to obsessive perfectionism, as with his devastating Clare Quilty in Stanley Kubrick's *Lolita* (1962) or his trio of appearances, each bafflingly different, in the same director's *Dr. Strangelove* (1964), it was grudgingly admitted as a price to pay for 'genius'. Following a virtually unbroken run of critical and commercial disasters during the sixties and seventies – films on occasion not even released – his colleagues grew less patient, particularly when, after his first heart attack in 1962, he gave a tactless anti-Hollywood interview.

Though Sellers became one of the highest-paid actors in the world with the creation of Inspector Clouseau, the accident-prone, tongue-tied sleuth of Blake Edwards' *Pink Panther* cycle, his powers of observation had visibly coarsened; and it was to general surprise that he ended his career with one of his most memorable performances, in Hal Ashby's *Being There* (1979), as Chauncey Gardnerm, a hypnotically placid bubble floating over Washington and ever about to burst. There was something both apt and disturbing about an actor who had confessed to his own lack of identity finally, and hauntingly, breathing life into a psychological nonentity.

They were, however, masterpieces of a quintessentially national character. *Listen to Britain*, for instance, was a sort of collage juxtaposing, in radio-fashion, images of potent, mythical Britishness: R.A.F. Spitfires bisecting a landscape by Constable, dancers on a packed ballroom floor in Blackpool, a BBC studio, the Houses of Parliament, infants playing in a schoolyard, a Myra Hess recital at the National Gallery. Why were such images so inaccessible to the non-Briton? Why should this film, like the rest of Jennings' work, be virtually unknown in Europe and the United States?

It is, basically, a matter of values. Blackpool Tower, in Jennings' eyes, constituted a *value* – which is to say, it went beyond architectural, aesthetic and social considerations to enter the pure realm of the symbolic. Leni Riefenstahl, his Nazi counterpart, restricted the subjects of her twin documentaries, *Triumph of the Will* (on the 1934 Nuremberg Party Convention) and *Olympiad* (on the 1936 Berlin Olympic Games), to glamourously ideal specimens of Aryan humankind. Jennings, on the other hand, had a true democrat's indifference to hierarchies – of rank, ability and physical allure. His subjects' names were not so much pseudonyms as 'anonyms', so to speak, classless names like Bill and Tom and Fred and Jacko. A miner scrabbling at a sodden, ill-lighted coal face could epitomise the British spirit as evocatively as Myra Hess at the piano – and was therefore, as a symbol, just as valuable and beautiful. And as urgently in need of protection. For, during the war, all that indomitable, threadbare British ordinariness was under siege, a siege investing it for Jennings with a topicality which appeared paradoxically *nostalgic*. His were British films meant exclusively for, and as affectionate tributes to, his beleaguered compatriots, without the selectively and compromise which result from angling after an international audience. In an unpejorative sense, he was preaching to the converted, except that Jennings never preached.

'I wouldn't take the advice of a lot of the so-called critics on how to shoot a close-up of a teapot.'
DAVID LEAN

Very different from Jennings were the august director-knights (as one speaks of actor-knights) of the British cinema: Sir David Lean, Sir Carol Reed and, gratefully honoured in both capacities, Sir Laurence Olivier. Not that, in the thirties and forties, when first heard of, any of these names was so prestigiously prefixed; yet knighthood as an outcome must always have appeared a distinct possibility. Theirs was a cinema By Appointment, as there are marmalades and cornflakes and deerstalker caps By Appointment. Indelibly academic in texture, though by no means lacking in narrative verve, the films of Lean, Reed and Olivier differed from Jennings' classics of sometimes slightly fey introversion not least in the ambassadorial confidence with which they projected suitable images of Britain around the globe.

(Above) David Lean on the set of *Oliver Twist* (1948); and (right) the Silver Prince of British film-making on location for *A Passage To India* (1985.)

As a director, Lean was the protegé of Noël Coward, himself a commanding presence in the cinema as performer, scenarist, composer, co-director, producer and indefatigably sophisticated *éminence mauve*. Their most celebrated collaboration was *Brief Encounter*, made in 1945, from a one-act play by Coward, and starring Trevor Howard and Celia Johnson. This, arguably the most esteemed of all British films, boasts an unexpected structural affinity with Luis Buñuel's *Le Charme Discret de la bourgeoisie* (a title applicable to much of Coward's work for the theatre and cinema) in that its narrative is articulated essentially through a series of *interruptions*. Frustrated partly by the mundane pressures of suburban routine and partly by their own self-repressions, Coward's forlorn middle-class lovers-to-be never quite consummate their bashful courtship. They are even denied the melancholy luxury of a protracted leave-taking, being interrupted by a defiantly gossipy neighbour. Which is why *Brief Encounter* is still a pivotal work for the British

cinema: it confronted directly, if a mite slickly, all that spinsterish good taste to appropriate it as a theme. Seldom has any film so dishearteningly conveyed the impression of lives atrophying from loyalty to a set of needlessly censorious values; of feelings preserved, like rock cakes, under a tea-shop bell jar; of emotional deadness, objectified here by the films's artful banality of dialogue, its greyness of setting, even by what François Truffaut once disparagingly referred to as the unexciting 'asymmetry' of British facial features. And if it now seems rather less than the masterpiece hailed by critics at the time, that may be due to one's sense of the narrative as condescendingly founded on a typical Cowardian conceit. What if, one fancies the Master gleefully musing in his silken dressing-gown, what if I invented lovers who *never* made physical love, who did *not* conduct their affair against exotic backdrops, who were *not* conventionally photogenic, etc.

Lean's pair of Dickens adaptations, *Great Expectations* (1946) and *Oliver Twist* (1948), further enhanced his reputation – and, in truth, they stand up marvellously well. I intend as an unambiguous compliment comparing them to the finest of Disney's feature-length cartoons, *Snow White*, for instance, or *Pinocchio*. Certainly, there is about them a density of visual texture savouring of Disneyesque animation, with the screen dissolving into near-abstract pools of light and shadow to suggest a preternatural vividness of villainy and terror.

Of his later inflationary period (a waggish showbiz adage put it nicely: 'Inside every Lean film there's a fat film screaming to get out') the most fascinating if perverse product was *Lawrence of Arabia* (1962), because, like his dreamily equivocal hero, Lean himself became enamoured of the desert, of the glinting harmonies of sun and sand and steel. For once the British cinema's waspish, white-haired Silver Prince (to borrow a locution from Tom Wolfe) threw off the dubious mantle of 'brilliant technician' and obsessively set to burrowing right inside his material. It was the absence of any such personal involvement which made *Doctor Zhivago* (1965) and *Ryan's Daughter* (1970) appear finally so insubstantial, however extravagantly budgeted and panoramically filmed. In fact, their blandly frontal pictorialism felt sometimes so like riffling through postcards that one fantasised finding, on the reverse side of the screen, the neatly printed name and address of the intended recipient alongside a giant scrawled message ending with 'Wish you were here'.

Carol Reed, with whose name Lean's has often

(Left) Omar Sharif, Peter O'Toole and the desert in Lean's *Lawrence of Arabia* (1962). (Top right). David Lean and Peter O'Toole meet Queen Elizabeth at the royal première of *Lawrence of Arabia*. (Bottom right) A pensive Carol Reed.

been linked, was a somewhat less assuming figure, less inclined to treat celluloid as worshipfully as though it were the twentieth century equivalent of marble. Reed, who entered the industry as a dialogue director, graduated to his own first feature in 1935. The most memorable of his early films – *Bank Holiday* (1938), *The Stars Look Down* (1939), *Night Train to Munich* (1940), *Kipps* (1941) and *The Young Mr. Pitt* (1942) – were prosaic, well-acted, technically proficient and, at best, stylish rather than made in any wholly individual style. His latter 'international' period – *Trapeze* (1956), *The Key* (1958), *The Running Man* (1963) and *The Agony and the Ecstasy* (1965, with Charlton Heston, as Michelangelo, climbing down from the Sistine Chapel ceiling as though from Mount Sinai) – consisted mostly of 'titanic' works supposedly built to last for ever but which sank on their maiden voyage. (Only his prettified, and much-parodied,

(Above) Vienna,
Greeneland: Orson Welles
as Harry Lime in Carol
Reed's *The Third Man*
(1949). (Top right) Salvador
Dali sketching Laurence
Olivier as Richard III; and
(bottom right) a younger
Olivier with Vivien Leigh
and Flora Robson in *Fire
Over England* (1937).

Dickens musical *Oliver!* afforded him, in 1968, a real commercial success). It is, then, on just three films from the late forties that his (in certain quarters) still quite considerable reputation is staked.

Of these *Odd Man Out* (1947) has cruelly dated. An account of a fatally wounded Irish gunman, played by James Mason, staggering through the night until shot down by the police, it suffers from the sort of over-studied effect announcing, even to those ignorant of the exact function of a director, that *here is a film which has been directed:* weirdly warped angles; sinisterly underlit faces; and the screen afflicted with regular bouts of the D.T.s. But *The Fallen Idol* (1948) and *The Third Man* (1949), both adapted from his own novellas by Graham Greene, found Reed at his most brilliant – in, respectively, a painful romantic drama and an 'entertainment', to employ Greene's familiar distinction. *The Fallen Idol*, about an ambassador's only (and lonely) child who finds himself privy to a surreptitious affair being carried on inside his father's Belgrave Square embassy, managed to sidestep the smeary melodramatics into which a less naturally prudent director might have steered it; and the performances from Ralph Richardson, Michèle Morgan and little Bobby Henrey were poignantly lifelike. As for *The Third Man*, Reed achieved a hole-in-one with it. It was an atmospheric, wonderfully well-paced thriller, a few of whose set-piece tableaux have become 'standards', as one says of popular songs: the very first, zither-accompanied apparition of Orson Welles' Harry Lime, stepping forth from out of a dark doorway with a satanically bemused smile on his seraphic features; his oft-quoted putdown of Switzerland aboard a Ferris Wheel in Vienna's Prater park; the sweaty climactic pursuit through that city's sewers; and, of course, the famous last, long-held shot of Alida Valli pitilessly, unforgivingly, cutting Joseph Cotton dead at Lime's funeral.

A final, rather subdued excursion into Greeneland, *Our Man in Havana*, released in 1959, with Alec Guinness, Noël Coward, Maureen O'Hara and Burl Ives, flickeringly reanimated the ironic absurdism of *The Third Man*, but the conclusion of Reed's career was, on the whole, a sad one.

It was perhaps Laurence Olivier's purpose, in filming *Henry V* (1944), *Hamlet* (1948) and *Richard III* (1955), that Shakespeare be apotheosised as England's foremost *living* dramatist. The Bard had been filmed before, often. But Olivier's adaptations transcended the hammy theatricality of those earlier attempts, with courtiers tactfully taking their leave

STARS OF THE FORTIES

'I have been No.2 in pictures for donkey's years. There are an awful lot of stars around who will do anything for lolly and laughs. I consider that it is professional whoredom to inflict a load of rubbish on to a paying public – and that is what too many actors are doing. The thing is I won't lower my sights. A film may turn out to be rubbish, but that's not always one's fault. Acting has to be fun for me, you see. Not work. I'm lazy. I hate work.'
TREVOR HOWARD

'I have no illusions about myself. I am a second-rate feature actor. I am not a star and never was – even in the old Rank days. I lack the essential spark, you see. But I have lived a fairly eventful life and met a lot of people both in and out of the acting profession, so I feel I have something to offer.'
DENNIS PRICE

'I'm not changing my name. Remember that I have won a certain reputation with it, and I don't feel like beginning over again with a fresh name. Besides, my real name sounds even crazier. I was christened Georgette Lizette!'
GOOGIE WITHERS

'If there is one thing calculated to intrigue film people it is to tell them that you are not especially interested in making pictures. It is a point of view they simply do not understand. They think you must be either a fool or a genius. In either case they feel they cannot forget you.'

'If I were writing my own obituary I would think that the thing to say about me is that I am versatile: I sing; I have appeared in cabaret; I have been, and I hope I still am, a popular film star; I have acted in some pretty intellectual pieces and in Shakespeare, but I have also made very commercial films; I have written plays and I have lectured on acting.'
MICHAEL REDGRAVE

'In the eyes of American journalism I have several doubtful attributes: I am a film star, I am undeservedly successful, and I an ENGLISH. I am not a case of a British star being taken for a ride in Hollywood. Some of the artists from this country who have been suffering an eclipse over there had been far too much typed as English characters. But not me. It was never my intention to export my costume film, or even *Seventh Veil*, personality from England.'
JAMES MASON

Laurence Olivier and Vivien Leigh in *Fire over England* (1937).

just as a soliloquy appeared imminent and blood-stained monarchs sporting what looked like bejewelled mediaeval ashtrays on their heads. And he was to be filmed again, no less often, and on occasion more cinematically (e.g. Kurosawa's *Throne of Blood*, Welles' *Chimes at Midnight*). Olivier's, however, had the merit of establishing a kind of mainstream 'authenticity', by which other, freer versions could be measured. They also served as enduring records of the director's own title performances, most notably his definitive Crookback; and *Henry V*, with its unmissable relevance to the embattled realities of 1944, was in its way blank verse propaganda.

His last and feeblest work as a director, *The Prince and the Showgirl* (1957), reflected a well nigh universal taste for British Royal Family gossip, as *Henry V* had reflected national solidarity during the Battle of Britain – a fair indication of its diminished ambition. Olivier himself was no match for his co-star, the almost supernaturally radiant Marilyn Monroe; and the film's failure was of the kind that makes every single critic in the world think of flat champagne and unrisen soufflés.

> **‘I don't believe in producers who put themselves up as impresarios and try to gather around them as many well-known names as possible. I personally always look for people whose ideas coincide with mine and am always ready to give them a chance to make a name for themselves.’**
> MICHAEL BALCON

(Opposite page) The American dramatist Arthur Miller, his wife Marilyn Monroe, Vivien Leigh and her husband Laurence Olivier snapped in 1956 during the shooting of *The Prince and the Showgirl*. (Top) Alec Guinness, far from Lavender Hill, with a youthful Audrey Hepburn and William Fox in *The Lavender Hill Mob* (1951). (Bottom) The ladykiller and the lady: Guinness and Katie Johnson during the filming of Alexander Mackendrick's *The Ladykillers* 1955.

With Ealing's comedies enjoying such autonomous celebrity, it tends to be forgotten just how many dramas, thrillers and assorted genres were produced by the studio, even during the administration of Michael Balcon. A handful of evocative titles may be cited: the portmanteau fantasy *Dead of Night* (1945); *The Overlanders* (1946), a spacious semi-documentary account of a wartime cattle evacuation across Australia; *The Loves of Joanna Godden* (1947), an Edwardian drama set on Romney Marsh; the splendidly titled costume melodrama *Saraband for Dead Lovers* (1948); *Scott of the Antarctic*, the 1948 Royal Command Performance film for which Vaughan Williams composed a sumptuous soundtrack score; and a pair of African extravaganzas, *Where No Vultures Fly* (1951) succeeded by *West of Zanzibar* (1954), both of them shot in glorious Localcolor.

Yet Ealing in its heyday monopolised British humour with such breezy aplomb that innocent filmgoers still confuse the two terms. The high regard in which these, when all is said and done, modest little films are held internationally (*Whisky a gogo!*, French for *Whisky Galore!*, is to this day a name much favoured for Parisian nightclubs) can no

(Below) Black and White: Alec Guinness as *The Man in the White Suit* with Howard Marion-Crawford and Michael Gough. (Top right) Ealing's supremo, Michael Balcon, visiting director Michael Truman and Jack Hawkins on the set of one of the studio's last comedies, *Touch and Go* (1955); and (bottom right) with Adriene Corri on the set of *The Feminine Touch* (1955).

MICHAEL BALCON

'We made films at Ealing that were good, bad and indifferent, but they were unmistakably British – they were rooted in the soil of the country. Ealing was a complete unit, a place where films were always in production. Now everything is so fragmented. Anyone with an idea can go to a production company, and if the company likes the 'package' – I mean the star, the gimmick and so on – they make it. Afterwards the thing breaks up, there's no continuity. This system produces now and again the outstanding film, but it doesn't produce a national style like, say, the Czechs.'

'The late Bernard Shaw, when informed that Sir George Somebody-or-Other was coming to tea and to have a conversation with him, replied: "Sir George has the power of speech, but not of conversation." It is essential, of course, that the film should have the power of speech; but equally it must have the power of conversation, in order to maintain its popularity.'

These two quotes succinctly define the approach to his chosen medium adopted by Sir Michael Balcon, arguably the single most influential figure in British film history. Balcon entered the industry as a regional distributor and, by the age of 27, had already produced his first feature, *Woman to Woman*, on which a youthful Alfred Hitchcock served as assistant director,

art director and screenwriter. Subsequently, he founded one of the most durable, commercially successful British studios, Gainsborough Films, and produced most of Hitchcock's classic thrillers of the period (including *The Man Who Knew Too Much*, *The Thirty-Nine Steps*, 1935, *The Secret Agent* and *Sabotage*, both 1936), as well as Robert Flaherty's *Man of Aran* in 1933. In 1931 he was appointed director of production at Gaumont-British and from 1936 filled the same post as MGM-British (from which studio emerged *The Citadel* an *Goodbye, Mr. Chips*).

Balcon's most celebrated achievement was unquestionably his twenty-two-year administration of Ealing Studios. Under his aegis the name 'Ealing' was to become, and not only in Britain, almost the generic term for English humour; and the studio's influence is evident in such recent comedies as Bill Forsyth's *Local Hero* and Richard Eyre's *Loose Connections* and *Laughterhouse*.

Even into the sixties, however, Balcon remained an active figure, founding Bryanston Films (responsible for *Tom Jones*, on which he was executive producer) and, following a much-publicized power struggle, taking over British Lion in 1964. Knighted in 1948, Balcon died in 1977. For better or worse, it can safely be claimed that, without his example, the phrase 'British film history' would now conjure up a very different set of images.

doubt be ascribed to the fact that they project an image of Britain such as foreigners, Americans in particular, fondly imagine it to be: essentially more rustic than urban, dotty but indomitable, with Will Hay as resident stationmaster, Margaret Rutherford as postmistress and Stanley Holloway propping up every available bar. Though commentators have focused attention on the importance, in the series, of what might be called an ideology of smallness, the curiously satisfying snugness of many traditional Ealing comedies was based, not so much on smallness in itself, as on *reduction*, on a calculated and ingratiating miniaturisation of the world. Thus, in *Hue and Cry* (1947), law enforcement is reduced to a mere make-believe frolic for children; in *Passport to Pimlico* (1949), the metropolis is reduced to Pimlico; in *Whisky Galore!* (also 1949), Scotland is reduced to a single inebriate offshore island; in *Kind Hearts and Coronets* (1949 yet again), parricide is reduced to a dandified aristocratic sport not unlike fox-hunting; in *The Titfield Thunderbolt* (1953), the nation's railway system is reduced to one quaint branch line; and, in the last of the breed, *Barnacle Bill* (1957), a chronically seasick sea-captain finds his command reduced to a dilapidated seaside pier.

Note, also, as a symptom of Ealing's influence, that the same effect of shrinkage can be detected in several comedies not issued by the studio; *Genevieve* (1953), in which the highway speed limit is dramatically reduced; *The Smallest Show on Earth* (1957), which reduces the cinema itself to fleapit pro-

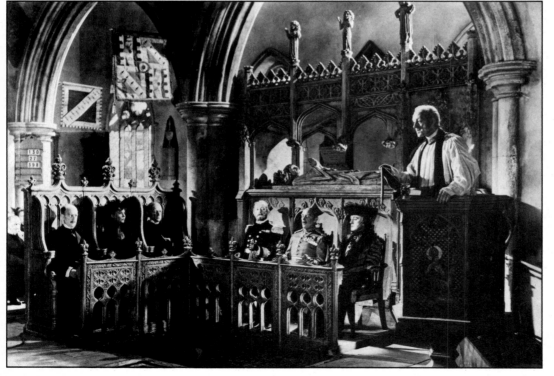

(Above) Kay Kendall's trumpet voluntary in *Genevieve* (1953). (Left) One for the Book of Records: the ubiquitous Guinness in Robert Hamer's *Kind Hearts and Coronets* (1949). (Opposite left) George Benson and the girls in Launder and Gilliat's *The Pure Hell of St. Trinian's* (1960); and (opposite right) Ian Carmichael and some naked ladies in the Boulting's *I'm All Right, Jack* (1959).

portions; even *The Mouse That Roared* (1959), a title irresistibly conjuring up a chronicle of the British cinema as 'The Lion That Squeaked'. Latterly, a neo-Ealing throwback such as Richard Eyre's *Laughterhouse* reduces the epic cattle drive of Howard Hawks' *Red River* to the footling caper of walking fattened geese to Smithfield Market.

There have been all kinds of glib and fascinating theories to account for the staunchly parochial populism typical of the Ealing formula in the forties and fifties. (In his interesting study, for instance, Charles Barr suggests that *The Ladykillers* – who, if you recall, abuse the hospitality of dear little Katie Johnson's Kings Cross maisonette – might represent 'the post-war Labour government taking over 'the House''.) So it is with a certain diffidence that I propose the following analogy. The Britain whose traditions were espoused by Korda was an imperial Britain, a Britain which saw itself impregnating every corner of the globe with its manly seed – a Britain, in a word, *erect*. That bequeathed to Balcon, however, was in the agonising process of withdrawing from those far-flung reaches of the Empire and inexorably curling in upon itself. And perhaps it would not be too fanciful to equate the wilful 'Little England' attitudes of most Ealing comedies with the sad, wrinkled shrivel of *detumescence*. (What this implies for the recent revival of its house-style – in *Local Hero*, *Loose Connections* and *Water* – does not bear thinking about.)

Of the directors whose reputations were made or consolidated at Ealing, only two, Robert Hamer and Alexander Mackendrick, truly developed styles distinct from that of the studio. Hamer was an unfulfilled, slightly melancholic talent, with a dry Francophile cast of mind and an aphorist's way with language (it seems almost a pity for the witticisms of *Kind Hearts and Coronets* to be thrown away on a

form as ephemeral as spoken dialogue, and one would like to be the film's Boswell, as it were, taking it all down). His two early exercises in polished seediness, *Pink String and Sealing Wax* (1945) and *It Always Rains on Sunday* (1947), showed real promise, but it was his misfortune not to be born French. Mackendrick was a Scot who directed *Whisky Galore!* and, also in his homeland, *The Maggie* (1953), as well as the more abrasive *The Man in the White Suit* (1951) and *The Ladykillers* (1955, with its black humour nicely counterpointed by the shiny textures of British Technicolor, whose overall tonality would seem to take its cue from the primary red of London's buses). Having quit Ealing, he made just four more films. Two of them, though, were arguably his finest: the squalid, glitzy *Sweet Smell of Success* (1957, with Burt Lancaster and Tony Curtis); and, in 1963, a quite subtle adaptation of *A High Wind in Jamaica*, Richard Hughes' Peter Panlike fable of ruthless children and put-upon pirates. Thereafter he was appointed dean of the film department of the Californian Institute of the Arts.

It might be worth casting an eye on some other toilers in the British comic tradition, most of whom came in twos, curiously, and all of whom were actively employed well into the seventies.

Frank Launder and Sidney Gilliat were least in thrall to the insatiable jokiness of the breadwinning professional humourist; but, though they alternated assignments as producer and director, it would take a lynx-eyed buff to be able to distinguish one from the other. A representative selection from their dual filmography would have to include *The Happiest Days of Your Life* (1950), *Folly To Be Wise* (1952) and *The Belles of St Trinian's* (1954), directed by Launder; *The Rake's Progress* (1945), *Green For Danger* (1946) and *Only Two Can Play* (1961), by

(Left) Dirk Bogarde and Kenneth More in a subtly humorous scene from Ralph Thomas's *Doctor in the House* (1954). (Right) Robert Shaw and Richard Todd at the controls in Michael Anderson's *The Dam Busters* (1955.).

Gilliat. Their collaboration has left us with a memory of unfailing good humour – in both senses of the term – and an occasional brainy prankishness.

The terrible twins of British comedy, the Boulting Brothers, actually began their careers (or career) in a more sombre register with, most notably, an adaptation of Graham Greene's *Brighton Rock* (1947), in which Richard Attenborough made an indelibly loathsome hoodlum, and *Seven Days To Noon* (1950), a calendrically eccentric title for a very gripping thriller about a crazed atomic scientist threatening to blow London up unless his demands are met. Of their low-humour, mean-spirited, self-styled 'satires' of Establishment institutions, the best was *I'm All Right, Jack* (1959), thanks in the main to Peter Sellers' mordant impersonation of a bolshie shop steward.

A mention, finally, of the Thomas brothers: Ralph, best-known for his 'Doctor' cycle (*Doctor in the House*, *Doctor at Sea*, etc.), which he would vary with melodramas that were not just mawk*ish* but downright *mawk;* and Gerald, perpetrator of the *Carry On . . .* series, now defunct, of ribald faces.

In the fifties our national cinema was a desert, frankly, of few oases (and most of these would turn out to be mirages). Though once regular attendances were already spiralling downwards from a wartime peak, the quantum leap affected by television sales in the mid-fifties provoked a precipitous decline which still, forlornly, waits to be reversed. Yet, aside from some sulky raillery at the new medium's expense (and Ealing went so far as to make an anti-TV comedy, *Meet Mr. Lucifer*, in the crucial Coronation year of 1953), and the implementation of the Eady Levy as a timorous governmental acknowledgement of imminent crisis, there appeared scant awareness within the industry that an art form which, from its cranky turn-of-the-century origins, had eclipsed in popularity all rival modes of representing 'reality' was beginning to experience acute public disaffection. No, producers produced, distributors distributed and exhibitors exhibited, as though with undimmed confidence that Ol' Man Public would just keep rolling along.

The never too inspiring product of the Rank Organisation, via its straitlaced 'charm school' of eternal starlets, soon regressed into featherbrained comedies with titles like *To Dorothy a Son* and *An Alligator Named Daisy*, the majority of which were adapted from West End stage hits. There were also inordinate quantities of war films of the 'stiff upper lip' brand, for which British directors and scenarists would wage the Second World War over and over again the way Sir C. Aubrey Smith, bristling with after-dinner bonhomie, used to lay out a pineapple to represent the Duke of Wellington, a bowlful of strategically positioned walnuts to represent the French troops and recreate the Battle of Waterloo for the umpteenth time. Commercially, several of these figured among the real successes of the domestic market – *The Cruel Sea*, *The Dam Busters* and *Reach For the Sky*. Aesthetically, they advanced the medium not an iota.

Rare endeavours to focus on a 'serious' theme were foredoomed by the usual triviality and pusillanimity. *Yield to the Night*, for instance, directed by J. Lee Thompson in 1956, caused quite a stir by choosing as its subject Ruth Ellis, the last Englishwoman to be hanged (and the protagonist of the recent, far superior *Dance With a Stranger*). But even if Diana Dors, the British cinema's resident sex symbol, with her chrome-gloss hair, her tawdry *volupté* and her masklike, floury white, unbreakably porcelain face – a face like a breast on which someone has pencilled a face – was oddly effective in a stagy, posturing fashion, the treatment seemed intent less on 'indicting' an unjust penal system than on voyeuristically leering at its heroine's degradation.

(Opposite page, top) Heave . . . Harry Andrews in *Ice Cold in Alex* (1958: the film's title is short for 'an ice-cold beer in Alexandria'). (Opposite page, bottom) . . . Ho! Jack Hawkins afloat on *The Cruel Sea* (1952). (Left) Christopher Lee in *Taste the Blood of Dracula*, directed by Peter Sasdy in 1969.

In commercial terms, the most successful film company in the British cinema has been Hammer, founded in 1948 by Will Hammer and Sir John Carreras, and getting into its stride with a sequence of low-budget horror films from the mid-fifties. For Hammer's admirers, *A Heritage of Horror*, David Pirie's account of the studio, is perceptively sympathetic. But if its output suffers in comparison with that, similarly based on horror (and science-fiction), of Roger Corman's spunkily inventive American International Pictures of the same period, it is no doubt because Corman's scouts, on the watch for cheap new talent, would lurk around the campuses of USC and UCLA like drug pushers outside some high school playground, while Hammer tended to rely, for its directors, on such perfectly competent but somewhat unexciting old hands of the industry as Terence Fisher and Freddie Francis. And what is slightly mysterious, given their immense popularity, is that these films, with Peter Cushing and Christopher Lee reinvoking the spirits of Frankenstein, Dracula, the Mummy and other weary campaigners of the genre, were not tremendously scary.

THE BRITISH TRADITION

'Probably all my work, even when it has been very realistic, has struggled for a poetic quality – for larger implications than the surface realities may suggest. I think the most important challenge is to get beyond pure naturalism into poetry.'
LINDSAY ANDERSON

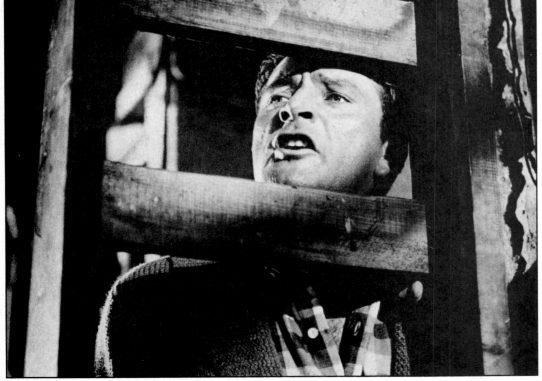

(Above) Shirley Ann Field amid the back-to backs of Karel Reisz's *Saturday Night and Sunday Morning* (1960). (Left) Richard Burton in Tony Richardson's *Look Back in Anger* (1959). (Opposite) Susannah York, Albert Finney and feathered friend in *Tom Jones*, adapted from Henry Fielding's classic novel by Tony Richardson and John Osborne.

It was in response to this climate of rampant commercialism, artistic mediocrity and vanishing audiences that the 'Free Cinema' movement evolved. Two of its advocates, Lindsay Anderson and Karel Reisz, had served as co-editors of the magazine *Sequence;* a third, Tony Richardson, was a notable TV producer and stage director; and all three were intimately associated with the postwar rise of the New Left. Their published manifesto, not a million miles away from Grierson's of twenty years previously, announced: 'Implicit in our attitude is a belief in freedom, in the importance of people and in the significance of the everyday'. In a subsequent interview, however, Reisz was more dispassionate: 'Those Free Cinema pictures acquired a very weird reputation: people talk about them as though they were polemical films, as though they were in some way political programme pictures – which they weren't. They were both over-rejected by the people who felt they were being attacked, and ludicrously over-praised by those who saw them as the beginning of a revolutionary culture. *Saturday Night and*

Sunday Morning, for example, is a very simple little tale about the sentimental education of a young man.'

The earliest and freshest of Free Cinema's documentary shorts – *Oh Dreamland, Momma Don't Allow, Every Day Except Christmas* and *We Are The Lambeth Boys* – did not neglect the movement's precepts (basically, getting the camera, like some pasty-complexioned, nose-in-a-book youth, *out of the house and into the open air*) and were akin to Cartier-Bresson photographs teased into animated life. And since they handily coincided with, and were much influenced by, an upheaval in the English theatre – with the kitchen sink replacing the french window as its emblematic prop – their first feature films effected a radical turnover in the performers who were to populate the British cinema. Out went Jack Hawkins, Kenneth More, Janette Scott and Sylvia Syms; in from the theatre came Albert Finney, Tom Courtenay, Rachel Roberts and Alan Bates. Therein, though, lay the problem. The Free Cinema revolutionaires resembled nothing so much as those German Bolsheviks whom Lenin scoffed at for law-abidingly purchasing platform tickets before proceeding to sabotage a train. Of all the movement's flagship films, often graced by fine performances and a gritty sense of detail, not one proved truly filmic in origin. They were based either on plays (Richardson's *Look Back in Anger*, 1959, and *The Entertainer*, 1960, both from John Osborne, and *A Taste of Honey*, 1961, from Shelagh Delaney; Reisz's charming *Morgan – A Suitable Case For Treatment*, 1966, from David Mercer; and John Schlesinger's *Billy Liar*, 1963, from Keith Waterhouse and Willis Hall) or novels (Jack Clayton's *Room at the Top*, 1958, from John Braine; Reisz's *Saturday Night and Sunday Morning*, 1960, from Alan Sillitoe; Richardson's *The Loneliness of the Long-Distance Runner*, his best film, 1962, from the same author's short story; Schlesinger's *A Kind of Loving*, also 1962, from Stan Barstow; and Anderson's *This Sporting Life*, 1963, from David Storey).

At their best, they recharged the British cinema's batteries with the dark energy of working-class themes and a greater candour in the handling of sexuality (aided by a concurrent relaxation of censorship). At the less persuasive end, they had a tendency to serve up thickly buttered slabs of pre-sliced life.

In any event, our cinema's egalitarian spasm was short-lived; by the mid-sixties Salford had ceased to be a fashionable address. Reisz, Richardson, Clayton and Schlesinger all packed their bags for internationally impersonal projects, where and when they could set them up – in Britain, if convenient. Anderson alone remained faithful to a genuinely 'British' tradition and, perhaps in consequence, completed only four features in almost two decades. The Free Cinema influence persisted on in a number of independent productions: notably, in Bill Douglas's trilogy set in a Scottish mining community, *My Childhood, My Ain Folk* and *My Way Home;* and, more obliquely, in two wonderfully strange and beautiful works by the film historian Kevin Brownlow, *It Happened Here* (1956, co-directed with Andrew Mollo), about a fictive Nazi invasion of England, and *Winstanley* (1975), a luminously severe account of the seventeenth century Digger revolt, whose exquisite black-and-white imagery made one feel, watching it, that colour processes had not yet been invented.

(Left) Kevin Brownlow's *Winstanley* (1975). (Right) J. Arthur Rank, the man *behind* the gong.

J. ARTHUR RANK

The actor James Mason commented tartly on J. Arthur Rank: "He is the worst thing that has happened to the British picture industry. Rank has so much money from his flour-milling business that he has been able to move in and absorb the whole industry. He makes the mistake of buying markets to expand his empire and he does not seem to care how much it costs. He has no apparent talent for cinema or showmanship. He surrounds himself with a lot of quaint folk who know nothing about the creative side of film-making." His biographer, Alan Reed, saw the man very differently: "If we ask why most people who know him will have come to like Arthur Rank, perhaps the underlying secret is that, in a fast-moving and mistrustful world, he was a man made genuine by a steadfast faith. Methodist principles may seem curious ones to guide the promotion of moving pictures but at least they gave J. Arthur Rank a considerable start over most other film promoters who had no principles at all." Finally, in an interview with the *Methodist Recorder* in 1942, Rank himself made this statement: "If I could relate to you some of my various adventures and experiences in the larger film world, you would not only be astonished, but it would, I think, be as plain to you as it is to me that I was being led by God."

It was in the mid-thirties, and as a result of his failure to find distribution for an explicitly religious film which he had produced, *Turn of the Ride*, that J. Arthur Rank, a member of a wealthy Yorkshire flour-milling family, determined to extend his control over not merely the production of films, but their

distribution and exhibition. By the end of the decade, therefore, he owned two of the three major distribution circuits in Britain, plus a number of studios and laboratories, a near-monopoly which he was to hold for almost three decades. During this period, the Rank Organisation, whose filmic logo – 'the man with the gong' – became one of the most cele-brated (and parodied) in the world, backed such productions as *In Which We Serve*, *The Way Ahead*, *Henry V*, *Odd Man Out*, *Caesar and Cleopatra*, *The Life and Death of Colonel Blimp*, *Brief Encounter* and *Blithe Spirit*, as well as its share of utterly forgotten thrillers, melodramas and farces.

By the fifties and sixties, Rank increasingly lost touch with the public's taste; and, though the company has retained its involvement in film production and distribution, its financial soundness is currently based on real estate acquisitions, bingo halls and ballrooms, and especially a hugely successful copying machine enterprise.

J. Arthur Rank himself was created a baron in 1957 and died in 1972.

JOSEPH LOSEY

Charles Laughton in the title role. Losey's half-dozen American films, though generally modest in their budgets, were already evident of a nervously dynamic shooting style and a gift for investing genre narratives with his leftist political concerns. Most notable among these were *The Lawless* (1950), *M* (1951, a remake of Fritz Lang's classic) and *The Prowler* (also 1951).

In Italy, shooting *Stranger on the Prowl* in 1951, he was summoned to testify before the House Un-American Activities Committee after being identified by a previous witness as a former Communist. Returning to the States, he discovered that he had already been blacklisted by the movie industry; and, realising that he was now unemployable in Hollywood, he settled in England, where he was obliged to direct his first few films under a pseudonym. In compensation for the trauma of exile, however, it was a series of British works which brought Losey to international attention: notably, *Blind Date* (1959), a taut thriller which totally revitalised the clichéd conventions of English 'realism'; *The Criminal* (1960), a powerful prison drama in a style made familiar from Warner Bros. in the thirties; and *The Damned* (1961), a strange and underrated science-fiction allegory.

Following a lavishly baroque excursion into international film-making with *Eva* (1962), set in a wintry Venice and starring Jeanne Moreau and Stanley Baker,

"I believe that the only thing that films can do is to illuminate human existence in terms of a particular observation on it and to distress, disturb and provoke people into thinking about themselves and certain problems. But NOT to give the answers."

Joseph Losey was unquestionably *the* major creative figure in the British cinema from the mid-fifties to the early seventies. Born, like the not wholly dissimilar Orson Welles, in Wisconsin, he early abandoned medical studies in favour of a stage and journalistic career. His theatrical reputation was established with the production of the 'Living Newspaper', a collage-like spectacle greatly influenced by Losey's mentor, the dramatist Bertholt Brecht, whose *Galileo Galilei* he famously produced in 1947 with

'I suppose if you keep telling a group of film-
makers that 'they are the most exciting, switched-
on, creative people working in their profession',
eventually some will believe it.'
RICHARD LESTER

Losey further enhanced his reputation by making a Pinter-scripted adaptation of Robin Maugham's study of corruption, *The Servant* (1963), in which Dirk Bogarde offered a brilliant performance as a valet who acquires a malevolent ascendancy over his weak-willed aristocratic master. Losey and Pinter were again to collaborate on *Accident* (1967) and *The Go-Between* (1971), the latter awarded the Golden Palm at the Cannes Film Festival.

Though his weaker films (*Boom!*, 1968, *Figures in a Landscape*, 1970, *The Romantic Englishwoman*, 1975), could fairly be described as a director's 'vehicles, in the sense that there are vehicles for actors or actresses, Losey's best work was distinguished by a brilliantly fluid camera style and – a lesson for any director concerned with the possibility of a properly indigenous film culture – an extraordinary ability to capture the essential of his films' settings. Unlike most of his British-born colleagues working at the same period, he contrived not only to film *in England*, but to *film England*.

In the early seventies, Losey based himself in France, where he made a number of somewhat over-elaborate 'international' productions. His last film, however, an adaptation of Nell Dunn's play *Steaming*, starring Vanessa Redgrave, was wholly British in origin; most unhappily, he died just after completing it in 1984.

(Above) Joseph Losey directing Wendy Craig and James Fox in *The Servant* (1963); and (left) Dirk Bogarde, James Fox and Sarah Miles in a scene from the same film. (Right) Monica Vitti on a stairway to nowhere in Joseph Losey's sixties fantasia, *Modesty Blaise* (1966).

The 'Swinging Sixties' – introduced to the cinema, curiously, by an adaptation of an eighteenth century novel, Tony Richardson's *Tom Jones* (1963) – enjoyed its brief moment. And most enjoyable from a sundry assortment of modish artefacts was Richard Lester's pair of Beatle extravaganzas, *A Hard Day's Night* (1964) and *Help!* (1965), book-ending *The Knack . . . And How To Get It* (also

(Opposite page) O'Toole and Burton in Peter Glenville's Becket (1963).

(Above) Rita Tushingham, Donal Donnelly and Albert Hall, three of the leading performers in Richard Lester's *The knack . . . And how To Get It* (1965).
(Centre) Julie Christie, the sixties' quintessential icon, in John Schlesinger's *Darling* (1965).
(Bottom) Sixties-iana from Michelangelo Antonioni's *Blow-Up* (1966).

71

1965, from Ann Jellico's play), each of them held aloft by its fidgety dazzle and airily choreographed hubbub. Lester, too, moved on to greener pastures; where he may have realised, in his skylarking progress, that while the public is pleased to detect, in the mature artist, the qualities of youth, it will no longer pardon the faults. In terms of its stylistics, the period has been survived only by the James Bond cycle, currently fielding two Bonds as there were once rival Popes, and the tuppence-coloured shockers of Ken Russell.

With that concluded, as such, the British tradition of this essay's title . . . temporarily, one has reason to hope. For though, in the seventies, the industry was active enough, how much of its output could be called British, in the sense of evincing tangible national characteristics? Were Stanley Kubrick's films 'British', except by convenience? Or Polanski's? Or Skolimowski's? Or even Nicholas Roeg's, British-born as he is? Was Antonioni's *Blow-Up* or Truffaut's *Farenheit 451* a British film? In fact, while Heathrow buzzed with the arrivals and departures of jet-setting film-makers (who prized in particular our special effects units), the domestic industry, as though resolved, equally and abjectly, to surrender to its twin Nemeses, Hollywood and the box, appeared to be pinning its faith on feature-length episodes of TV situation comedies.

Meanwhile, in his well-appointed office, a young advertising executive named David Puttnam . . .

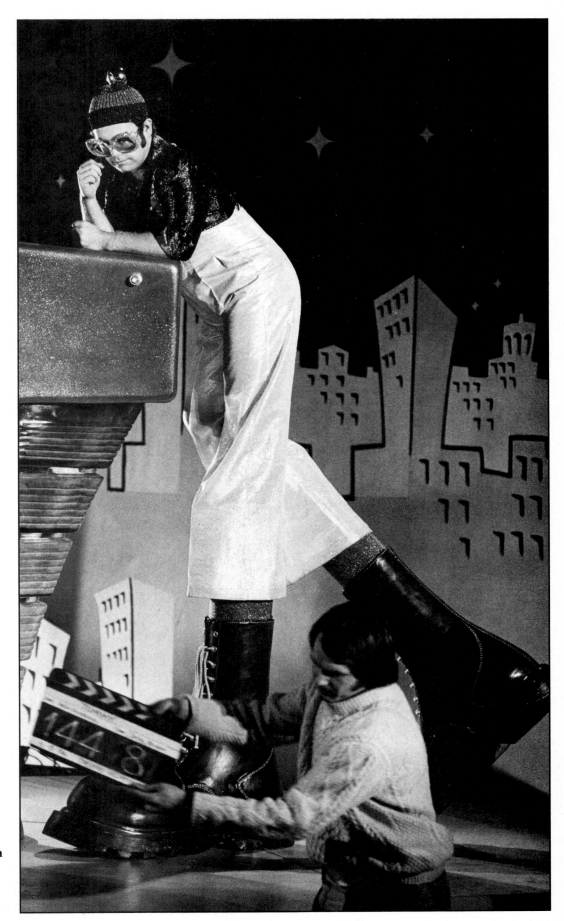

(Left) Oskar Werner and Julie Christie's *Fahrenheit 451* (1966); and (right) Elton John, a figure from the seventies, in Ken Russell's film version of the Who's 'rock opera' *Tommy* (1975).

THE BRITISH REVIVAL

Nick Roddick assesses the renaissance that started with the *Chariots of Fire* Oscars and the launching of Channel 4 and wonders about the future of British film-making.

PART TWO:
THE BRITISH REVIVAL
by Nick Roddick

Give someone an Oscar, put them in front of a bank of television cameras, and they are likely to come out with some pretty forgettable statements, mentioning mothers, producers, co-stars, members of the Academy and, if the compere doesn't cut them off first, God, their agent and the head of Universal Pictures. Three years ago, however, British writer and actor Colin Welland managed to be a little more memorable. Bounding out of the audience to accept an Oscar for the screenplay of *Chariots of Fire,* Welland showed the same talent for well-judged rhetoric that had made the film such a hit. 'The British,' he told the Los Angeles Music Center audience and the world's televiewers, 'are coming'.

If there is one moment at which the idea of a 'British film renaissance' really took shape, it is that Oscar night, 23rd March 1982. At long last the British film industry – for many years an institution which it had been fashionable to view with the same gloomy nostalgia as rural railway branchlines and bobbies on bicycles – was showing real signs of getting its act together. *Chariots of Fire,* the first British film to win the Best Picture Oscar since *Oliver!* in 1968 (and the first one ever to do so in anything approaching modern dress), was not only unmistakably British but also apparently commercial – the sort of dream ticket for which the British film industry had been groping around for years. By a quirk of history, Welland's statement also managed to anticipate the spirit of the times: a mere 48 hours after the Oscar ceremonies, General Galtieri's troops invaded the Falklands; and, whatever other effect

'The British are coming' called Colin Welland during *Chariots of Fire* Oscar night, 1982. To many, however, it seemed they had been 'here' for years.

this may have had, it certainly ushered in the biggest burst of British national feeling since World War II. Britain's national identity was being redefined after a period of extreme vagueness, and it was a good time for a national film revival.

The time was ripe in other ways, too. At the end of the previous year, the British treasury had followed the lesson of a number of Western countries, most notably Australia, in offering substantial tax concessions to anyone investing in film production. This, together with the success of *Chariots of Fire*, represented the culmination of a five-year process of confidence-building by British producers like *Chariots'* David Puttnam, aimed at persuading major British investors that film was a good place to put their money (though, ironically, *Chariots* had been funded by a combination of American and Egyptian capital). The third circumstance contributing to the revival had to do with the film industry's long-standing rival, television. With Channel 4, the country's first new television network for twenty years, due to go on the air in little over six months, the chances were increasing dramatically of getting small-to-medium budget features off the ground, often dealing with the sort of personal themes that had sustained continental European cinema since World War II, but which had been notably lacking from the British big screen.

All of this, however, could not really hide some of the ironies in Welland's brashly confident battle cry. In the first place, the sort of numbers who, from the comfort of their own homes, would have been watching Welland on the Oscar telecast, were the sort of numbers the British cinema had long since given up even dreaming about getting to hand over the price of a ticket at the box office. The other irony was that Welland's statement was made in Hollywood – a place (or, more properly, an industry) which had long enjoyed a one-way relationship with the British film industry. To many people, listening on that night, it must have seemed that the British weren't coming: they'd been there for years already. Many of the most striking American films of the past decade had been directed by emigré Brits, and many, many more had been designed, written, photographed or edited by them. With *Blade Runner* and *Flashdance* in the pipeline, the trend showed no signs of halting.

The lure of Hollywood has always been something that the British film industry has had to reckon with. Since the cinema is an industry as much as, if not more than, it is an art form, the ways in which film 'artists' work differ from the methods of a novelist or a painter. The latter, in the great tradition of the romantic poets, need only a garret and the barest minimum of equipment. Film-makers, on the other hand, need tens of thousands of pounds worth of equipment, tens of millions of pounds worth of film-making facilities, and production funds somewhere in between the two. In the past, the British economy and the British box office have repeatedly proved too limited to provide this on a regular basis, and British film-makers from Alfred Hitchcock in the thirties to Alan Parker in the seventies, have gone to Hollywood to make their films. But perhaps the nearest analogy for the cinema is not one of the other arts, but the sporting world, where British athletes will 'study' in the United States so as to avail themselves of the sporting facilities provided by American colleges (where sport, like the movies, is big business), but can still run for Britain in international competition. If those athletes qualify as British, why not the film-makers?

There is no easy answer to that question, but the fact that it springs so readily to mind is characteristic of the situation of the British cinema in the eighties. Certainly, other European countries periodically lose their key talents to the United States, but it is usually only a temporary loss: Wim Wenders from Germany, Bernado Bertolucci from Italy have 'gone Hollywood' and come back, with no real effect on the films they make back home. But, after fifty years of colonization by the American cinema, Britain's cinema is that much more vulnerable, mainly because of the fact that we share a language with our big transatlantic neighbour.

This, of course, is something that cuts both ways. If British film-makers have been able to make American films in a way that other European film-makers have not – the relative commercial failures of, say, Louis Malle's *Pretty Baby* and Wim Wenders's *Hammett* stem from the fact that they are not 'American' movies in the way that, say, Alan Parker's *Fame* and Michael Apted's *Coalminer's Daughter* undoubtedly are – it is because the dividing line between American films and British films has grown narrower and narrower over the years, a process accelerated by the penetration of British television by American series and serials. As Alan Parker puts it, looking back to his start in features, 'I'd written five screenplays, all of them very English, very London, very angry working class. If I'd just walked up and down Wardour Street trying to get those films made, I'd still be walking up and down. I had to think: what did I know about? And what I *did* know about was American movies.'

This has necessarily had a damaging effect on British film culture, because that is the area in which the Hollywood 'talent drain' has hit hardest. Like any form of culture, film culture, if it is to grow and develop, relies on the artist having a burning need for expression, and a fairly clear cultural tradition with which to interact. A French film-maker has only the French cinema in which to make French films (Belgium, Switzerland and French-speaking Canada have, after all, never posed any serious threat). British film-makers, committed though they may initially be to British film-making, necessarily find it hard to resist the inducements offered by Hollywood where, at a price, the need for self-expression can be fulfilled. Meanwhile, the chances of an indigenous film culture prospering are correspondingly weakened. So, too, are the chances for an investor to get his money back from a British film. With no tradition to support it, a British film is in a poor condition to compete against American films at the box office, especially since the latter are almost certain to have had more money spent on both production and marketing. It is a form of competition against which few British films – and few British film-makers – have been able to stand up, and thus the incentive to invest in British films is accordingly reduced. As with commerce, so with culture: there is no real *need* for a British cinema – or so it seemed before the *Chariots of Fire* Oscars gave the industry, and public awareness of it, a much-needed shot in the arm.

The shared language has also been responsible for compromising the other potential avenue of suste-nance for a national film industry: state support, direct or indirect, has never really amounted to anything much in Britain. Whereas other European countries, from Italy to Sweden, have seen that there is a need for state aid if national screens are not to be swamped by (dubbed) American movies, the British government has been content to do little more than tinker with the fringes of the film world, attempting to introduce a quota here, offering small-scale financial assistance there to films with a 'reasonable chance' of commercial success. What is more, the need for cinema to explore national themes has been diluted by the tradition of British television drama which, since the early sixties, has filled the cultural role which continental governments have been trying to promote through state support of their national film industries.

Not, of course, that the London-Los Angeles link has been an entirely negative one. The directors who have gone to Hollywood have generally returned, bringing with them new sets of skills and a new outlook on life – which, often, has been just what the British cinema, with its in-built tendency towards parochialism, has needed. To an even greater extent, the frequency with which world stars like Michael Caine, Sean Connery, Jacqueline Bisset and Maggie Smith, and world-class cinematographers like David Watkin and the late Geoffrey Unsworth have switched between Culver City and Pinewood, Burbank and Elstree, has done much to redress the balance.

The other major benefit to come to the British film industry by means of a 747 is not one that is

ALAN PARKER
Director

Alan Parker is probably the most successful of Britain's jumbo-jet directors – the ones who are as likely to make their films in Hollywood. From *Midnight Express* (1977) to *Birdy* (1985), Parker has more often worked 'on location' than at home. Occasionally attacked by British critics for not making his films British enough, he is not one to miss a chance to hit back.

'I always think of what I do as British,' he says of the Pinewood based Alan Parker Film Company. 'We're just a bunch of yobboes who got lucky, and what we do is, we go on location. We went on location to Malta to do *Midnight Express*, but it was a totally British crew. When we went to New York to do *Fame*, we had the same key personnel, and again in Northern California for *Shoot the Moon*. I wouldn't go if I didn't have these people, because they're the ones I make films with: we get on aeroplanes and go make movies somewhere else.

'What happens, though, is that I go on location for seven months to do *Fame*, and maybe six months for *Shoot the Moon;* then, when I come back, journalists write things like "Alan Parker, now back in this country after two years away . . ." It's nonsense! I've never left. My offices are here, at Pinewood, and I live in Richmond. It's just that, in order to do my job, I have to go on location.

'For instance, I want to do a film based on the Tom Sharpe novels. When I go to Africa to do that, I'll be on location. I won't have joined the African film industry.'

I'm sorry I didn't see your last films I can't stand kids in movies so I missed Bugsy Malone and I'm not into sado-masochism so I skipped Midnight Express and the reviews put me off Fame – all those winge-ing kids – but I did buy the leg warmers and 'Shoot the Moon' – well let's face it, you get enough of that at home without going to the movies and 'The Wall' well once I heard about him shaving off his eyebrows.. yuk.. But don't get me wrong I'm a big fan.. I loved those Joan Collins Cinzano commercials you did...

Alan Parker

immediately visible to the British cinemagoer, or indeed to cinemagoers anywhere. And yet it is one that, more than tax incentives and more even than the continued passion for film-making of a handful of dedicated people, has kept the British cinema alive through the dark years of the late sixties and seventies. It is the fact that Britain's major film facilities – the studios, the equipment hire companies, the processing laboratories and the technicians who work for all of them – have increasingly become a focus for Hollywood film-makers. Many of the block-busters of the past decade – the *Star Wars* series, the two Indiana Jones movies, *Reds* and the *Superman* cycle (which, between them, account for half of the top ten most successful movies of all time) – were made on the soundstages and backlots of the two major British studios, Pinewood and Elstree (with, increasingly, Twickenham, Shepperton and Wembley's Lee International getting their share of the work).

Of course, overseas studios have been popular with Hollywood before – Rome's Cinecittá in the fifties, the Samuel Bronston complex in Madrid in the sixties. But the British studios have already outlived both these fads, establishing themselves not merely as cheap places to make films – some of the biggest superproductions were, after all, based in Britain when the pound stood at over two dollars – but as an invaluable focus of know-how and facilities. For once, the shared language has acted to Britain's advantage, providing the British film industry with its one sure source of continuity and profit. Without it, the infrastructure of filmmaking, as vital to a national cinema as finance and passion, would have shrivelled and decayed, like our shipyards and our steel mills.

In a decade in which established British industries have, through a combination of mismanagement, lack of government interest and a general failure of long-term thinking, become the world's lame ducks, the British film industry (as opposed, sadly, to British film culture) has been one of the country's great unsung success stories. The viability of the whole undertaking is proved by something that happened in July 1984. Pinewood's giant '007 Stage' – named, obviously, after the Bond movies it had so often housed – was burned to the ground, shortly before the latest in the series, *A View to a Kill*, was to go into production. Within days, it was announced that the stage would be rebuilt and, in the process, improved. Six months later, on a bitterly cold day in January 1985, the new stage, renamed after the producer of the Bond movies, Albert R. 'Cubby' Broccoli, was reopened, in time for the obligatory Big Bond Set to be filmed on it. That sort of schedule, that sort of investment and that sort of commitment are scarcely the hallmark of a dying industry.

Britain, in other words, is a better place for film production than it may seem. There are the facilities, there are the skilled personnel and there is the equipment. But film production and a national cinema are not necessarily the same thing: and the problem is that the majority of the films made with those facilities aren't really British.

Defining a 'British' film is harder than it sounds. A French film, a Swedish film or a Japanese film are easy enough to spot. An American or an Australian film are determined by their country of origin. With a British film, however, it is not quite so straightforward. An English-language film is likely, nine times out of ten, to be American. And the country-of-origin test is not always reliable either. If it were, *Superman* would be a British film, because that is what is says on *Superman*'s certificate of registration. Yet its story, its stars and its setting are all

(Left, left and right) Alan Parker's *Bugsy Malone* (1976) and *Fame* (1980). 'I always think of what I do as British'. (Right) Michael Caine in *Educating Rita* (1983) and (below) *Water* (1985).

MICHAEL CAINE
Actor

Not since Cary Grant has a British actor achieved Hollywood stardom on the same scale as Michael Caine. After starring roles in British films like *Zulu* (1964), *The Ipcress File* (1965) and *Alfie* (1966), Caine settled in the United States, attracting a good deal of sniping from the British press. But anyone who knows Caine would not expect him to be apologetic: an actor whose professionalism is praised with almost embarrassing regularity by directors and fellow actors, he explained his attitudes while on location near his East End birthplace – it was actually meant to be Berlin – for his latest thriller, *The Holcroft Covenant*.

'Everywhere I lived,' he said, 'has been pulled down, so there's nothing left for me here: it's of no sentimental value to me at all. When I moved to America, although I missed England very much, for about six months I was walking round thinking, "there's something here that's rather nice and I don't know what the bloody hell it is!" Then I woke up one morning with the sudden brainstorm that I hadn't been bothered by the *class* thing for months. And I thought, "That's it!" That was rather pleasant. Like everywhere, of course, there are swings and roundabouts: you wind up in a classless society with a lot of people who don't have any class!

'But I live my life exactly how I please, and I certainly don't worry about what anybody else thinks or says as long as it doesn't affect me. The British press doesn't affect anybody in the United States, for the simple reason that no one reads it. And it doesn't affect me professionally, because the British don't go to the movies anyway. All it does if I become unpopular here, is it means less people pirate the video of the movie I'm in.'

DAVID WATKIN
Director of Photography

SPECIAL PRESENTATION

DOLBY STEREO

6 TRACK MAGNETIC SOUND

ANAMORPHIC PANAVISION

70 mm

Oh bugger we've forgotten the name of the film

Alan Parker

Does the future hold fewer 'quirkily British' films like *Kes* (top right) and more, geared to a world market, like *The Killing Fields* (bottom right)?

David Watkin, who shot *Chariots of Fire*, has divided his time between Britain and America, and between feature films and commercials. His most recent movies have been *Yentl*, made in England and Czechoslovakia with an American director, Barbra Streisand; *The Hotel New Hampshire*, shot in Hollywood for a British director, Tony Richardson; and *White Knights*, shot at Pinewood for an American director, Taylor Hackford. He claims to be equally at home with both systems, as he explained at Laird International Studios in Culver City, California, while shooting a car commercial for American television.

'I find it different, working in the two systems – equally enjoyable, but in different ways. There are some things out here that they do much better, and there are some things we do better over there: it's a method of approach.

'For example, in England, the electricians set the lamps, they set the flags' – metal sheets which block off part of the light from a spot – 'and they put up the reflectors. Out here, the job is divided between the electricians and what they call grips. The electricians will only set the lamps. If I want a flag on a lamp or a white reflector in front of it, that is done by the grips.

'Now, pros and cons: because it is the grips' job out here, they are very well organized and can get a bigger reflector up in half the time. It works terrifically well, *except* . . . it is also the grips' job to lay the tracks for the crane or the dolly. So, if you are suddenly setting up a big tracking shot or a big crane shot, I can set all the lamps, but I can't set any of the flags or reflectors!

'The other thing is, out here, there is a tendency for the Director of Photography to get very involved in lining up shots and set-ups, and to leave the Chief Electrician to light the shot. I think that's a bad system: the operator comes in at the very end and operates the shot, and the D.o.P. just sort of takes care of the artists.'

American: production just happens to have been based here. With *Midnight Express*, also registered as a British film, we get a little nearer to the heart of the problem: its director, producer, crew and quite a few of the cast were British, but its star and its story are American, and its setting is Turkey. Yet a definition cannot be devised to exclude it. Nor should one be. To take two random examples from very different eras, John Ford's *The Quiet Man* is indubitably American, for all its Irish setting, story and predominantly Irish cast. And Volker Schlöndorff's *Circle of Deceit*, though set in Lebanon, is very much a German film. In the final analysis, nationality tests on films are as meaningless, if not quite as odious, as tests for racial characteristics on people. Indeed, for any such system to work, there would need to some ludicrous sort of means tests equivalent – a required percentage of Cockney accents per film, perhaps, or a quota of big red buses.

The truth is, of course, that a healthy national cinema can afford to incorporate stories from abroad. Britain's national cinema, however, has never been that healthy; and it has, as a result, tended to be swamped by its overseas visitors. Nor is it hard to see why: there is, in the realm of British cinemagoing, little margin for error. For, if the film production industry in Britain has survived and even prospered since World War II, film distribution and exhibition have gone into a long and all but fatal decline. From the postwar boom period, when there was no television to speak of and Britons went to the cinema twice a week, annual cinema admission figures have dropped from around 1,500 million to 1984's figure of less than 50 million. This is deflation with a vengeance: today's figure is just over 3 per cent of the postwar one. Clearly, leisure habits change in half a century, but rarely that dramatically: the British, it seems, have all but given up going to the pictures. What this means for the production of British films is that the home market is almost negligible. To succeed, a British film has got to do so on the world – which, to all intents and purposes, means the American market if it is to stand any chance of getting its money back. Not only is the British market too small: on it, the competition from American films and from video is too intense.

This is a reality which can, of course, cut two ways: it can result in transatlantic films – the sort of film which, in the brief vogue for British production which followed the success of *Tom Jones* in 1963, sounded the death-knell of an earlier renaissance. Or it can lead to British films which are conceived for a world market – films which are commercial as well as distinctive, like *Chariots of Fire*. This is a crucial context into which the British film renaissance must be set, for it is the only way for the British film industry to survive on the free market onto which history and successive British governments have cast it. But it is a strategy which calls almost inevitably for producers to play it safe. The future is likely to see less films like *Morgan – A Suitable Case For Treatment* (1966) and *Kes* (1969) – quirkily British – and more like *Chariots of Fire* and *The Killing Fields*, cosmopolitan and geared to the world market. For all one's hopes for a British film renaissance that will be British in tone and content, the current world film scene and the appalling state of the British box office dictate a different reality. Britain, unlike almost any other country of comparable size and cultural history, has to make films for the world first; and for herself second. Perhaps this will prove an invaluable discipline: only time will tell.

With all the talk of a British film renaissance and the accompanying tendency to view *Chariots of Fire* as a kind of 'first' – an attitude which relegates pre-*Chariots* films to the status of steam-driven collectors' items – it needs to be stressed that the British film renaissance of the eighties did not come out of thin air.

The films came, in fact, as has already been suggested, out of an industry which, while it may have been short on indigenous product, was pretty well equipped with production machinery. They came, for all its uncertainties as far as cinema is concerned, out of the established cultural tradition of television drama and out of made-on-film commercials. They came out of the film schools, they came back from Hollywood and, in one or two rare instances, they came out of the woodwork of the alternative cinema.

This last area deserves a moment's attention, since the commitment on which it is based – political commitment, a belief in the need for cinematic experiment – has been able sporadically to sustain a tradition of alternative cinema in Britain since the thirties, producing films that the general public rarely sees, but which have had packed and lively screenings in student unions and art colleges, at political rallies, at festivals and, occasionally, in the BFI-funded regional film theatres.

More recently, alternative film-makers have ceased to be quite so firmly ostracized by the mainstream industry; since the film technicians' union, the ACTT, introduced its 'Workshop Agreement' in the early eighties, this kind of film-making has been brought a little further back into the mainstream fold. But it will never be entirely recuperated, nor should it wish to be. Its subject matter and its experimental approach occupy the position that the avant garde has always occupied in all art forms: a marginal but essential stimulus, occasionally an irritant, doing things that mainstream cinema can't or won't do, and ultimately feeding its results back into that mainstream.

Independent cinema in Britain, as elsewhere in the world, has belonged to two traditions – the politically active and the formally innovative – with frequent but not necessary overlaps. In the eighties, it has produced some striking works, seen at festivals in Britain and overseas – films like Barry Bliss's *Fords on Water* (1983), a deft piece of political future shock, with the current background of long-term unemployment as its starting point; Peter Wyeth's *Twelve Views of Kensal House* (1984), which fuses a documentary on what was, in the

Peter Greenaway's *The Draughtsman's Contract* (1983) had the largest audience of any avant garde film in British history. Even those who found it precious and pretentious admired its elegant look and feel.

LEON CLORE
Producer

Leon Clore is one of the senior producers of the British cinema. After working his way up through the departments and spending some time on documentaries, he has produced two of Karel Reisz's most successful films, *Morgan – A Suitable Case For Treatment* (1966) and *The French Lieutenant's Woman* (1981). Clore survived the dark ages of the seventies to see his biggest production, *The French Lieutenant's Woman,* eclipsed in the Oscar nominations and awards by *Chariots of Fire.* His views on the chances of a British film renaissance, expressed here the week after the 1983 Oscars, are fairly sanguine.

'The English,' he says, 'have never been a race of cineastes. I suppose one of the reasons is that they haven't had the variety of films you get on the continent, primarily because we speak the same language as the Americans. If the United States had spoken Spanish, there would have been an indigenous British film industry.

'Also, to be fair, we probably have the best television in the world, and, more than any other country in the world, television keeps people away from the cinema in England. If you lived in some European countries, there would be nothing to keep you at home.'

Clore is quite happy to see the Hollywood superproductions being filmed in England. 'They create employment. But they are actually American films; and there is a need for indigenous films. *Chariots of Fire* and *The French Lieutenant's Woman* are indigenous British films, even if they are financed by Americans. I've always been a believer that British films do best in America when they are most indigenous. We *need* the indigenous ones, and we have to find a way of continuing to make them.'

Now.. you're absolutely sure you're a friend of David Puttnam's..

Alan Parker

thirties, a model housing development in West London, with Wyeth's ongoing inquiry into how truth and history can be conveyed on film; Jan Worth's *Doll's Eye* (1983), a similar combination of an inquiry into prostitution with the traditions of experimental cinema; or Ken McMullen *Ghost Dance* (1983), the nearest thing the British cinema has yet produced to the intriguing, maddeningly discursive experiments of the French New Wave.

Occasionally, a film-maker from this tradition will make a temporary incursion into the mainstream, as Peter Greenaway did with his enormously successful *The Draughtsman's Contract* (1983), funded by the British film institute and seen more widely than any British avant garde film in history. Mostly, though, this is a tradition that glories in its marginality, as with one of its most fascinating products, *Carry Greenham Home* (1983), a video made by two first-year students at the National Film and Television School, Beeban Kidron and Amanda Richardson, who simply took a video camera and a tape recorder to the women's anti-nuclear peace camp at the US Air Force base at Greenham Common and, in a little under 70 minutes, provide what the assembled forces of the world's media failed to come up with in two years of intensive reporting – a clean, unromanticized but not uncritical portrait of one of the key phenomena of the eighties. As long as Britain's alternative cinema can come up with work like *Carry Greenham Home*, it should never be discounted. And it is important to realise that, though it will almost certainly not be celebrated, it is as much a part of British Film Year as the *Gandhi*s and the *Passage to India*s.

In terms of commercial success and artistic acclaim, no film was more symbolic of the British film renaissance than *Gandhi* (1983), which set an all-time record for a British film by winning eight of that year's twelve major Oscars.

Nor was *The Draughtsman's Contract* the only successful crossover to the mainstream. In 1983, there was another, much less publicized Oscar than those for *Chariots of Fire* and *Gandhi:* the one won by the working partnership of director James Scott and producer Christine Oestreicher for Best Short Film with *A Shocking Accident*. Scott was one of the stalwarts of the radical Berwick Street Collective in the sixties and early seventies and, though *A Shocking Accident* is too brief for it to be apparent, his subsequent longer film, *Every Picture Tells a Story* (1984) (again produced by Oestreicher), which is a fascinating dramatic biography of Scott's father, a painter, reveals how the concerns and strategies of the independent cinema can regenerate the side currents of the mainstream.

A similar source of new energy has been the world of television documentary, generally far more radical than television drama and certainly more so than television light entertainment. It has been easier for women film-makers to train in this area than in the traditional industry, with its in-built tendency (defended in the name of efficiency) to cast women as production assistants, continuity girls [sic] and,

occasionally, film editors. The last couple of years has seen the emergence of a number of first-class feature producers and directors, like Dee Dee Glass and Barbara Rennie, producer and director respectively on 1984's *Sacred Hearts* (on which the director of photography, Diane Tammes, was also a woman), and Mary McMurray, directing her debut feature in 1985, *The Assam Garden* (with veteran British star Deborah Kerr returning to the big screen for the first time in fifteen years), after a ten-year career in television.

But it is, obviously, the more mainstream efforts that have caught the world's attention and that have resulted in the 'British film renaissance' label. With very, very few exceptions, none of Britain's film-makers of the eighties have followed the traditional old-fashioned road to directing features – up through the industry, from runner to editor to assistant to director: the sort of route followed by earlier directors like David Lean and Jack Clayton. They have come, rather, from the Film School, often via documentary and information films; and, more recently, from the booming, noisy, volatile world of promo videos.

CHRISTINE OESTREICHER AND JAMES SCOTT

Christine Oestreicher and James Scott live and work together in a large, pleasant house in a square in Islington. They met in 1977, when Oestreicher, who already knew Scott's film work, was working on a book of interviews. They talked about making it into a film, then Oestreicher agreed to collaborate on Scott's next film, *Chance, History, Art* . . . (1980), made for the Arts Council.

Out of that collaboration has come Flamingo Pictures, whose output includes two distinctive shorts, *Couples and Robbers* and the Oscar-winning *A Shocking Accident*, and the feature, *Every Picture Tells a Story*, premiered at the 1984 London Film Festival.

Says Scott, 'there was always a limitation on the showing of Arts Council films, but I think I did a film that actually broke through that – the Richard Hamilton film – that got a lot of showings: it was shown on the BBC and internationally on television. I think that was because it was a popular film, whereas films that are considered 'intellectual' are limited to a particular market. It's important that those films get made, and that they are seen by the audiences they're for. It's just that my own inclination is to make films that are more popular or entertaining.'

'I like the idea of making subjects which would other-

wise perhaps not have been done,' says Oestreicher, pursuing the point, 'but of making them accessible to a wider audience. With *Every Picture*, that's what we're trying to do. With my book of interviews, I was trying to do that – trying to make accessible a subject that's been treated in a very intellectual way.

'But, with the films, a point came when we realised that, instead of trying to knock our heads against the wall and make the interview film, we should actually go back to square one and get something on the major circuits, which is why we made *Couples and Robbers*.'

(Left) Oscar winner (Best Supporting Actress) Dame Peggy Ashcroft as Mrs. Moore, with Victor Banerjee as Aziz in David Lean's *A Passage to India* (1985). (Below left) Victor Banerjee and James Fox in a passage to an Oscar nomination for Best Film of 1984. (Below right) Judy Davis as Adela, James Fox as Fielding: would E. M. Forster have approved?

Not, of course, that the old guard itself ceased to be a part of the British cinema scene in the eighties: both Jack Clayton and David Lean had films released (one with a great deal more success than the other), and such younger 'veterans' as Ken Russell, Lindsay Anderson, Karel Reisz, John Schlesinger, Tony Richardson and John Boorman have remained active.

Clayton, a skilled craftsman who, with *The Innocents* in 1961, showed himself to have more than just a touch of genius, finally recovered from the debacle of *The Great Gatsby* (1974) to undergo an even more debilitating experience with *Something Wicked This Way Comes* (1982). A potentially stylish horror thriller based on the Ray Bradbury story, the film bears all the marks of disastrous interventions and muddled thinking by the Disney Studio, which produced it (and which, at the time, was going through a particularly bad patch).

David Lean, of course, came back after an even longer break – his last film had been *Ryan's Daughter* in 1970 – for the multi-Oscar nominated *A Passage to India* (1984). Lean's film (which was edged out of the Awards by *Amadeus*) is very much the work of Britain's longest established *auteur*, since he wrote and edited it as well as directing it. For all the bustle and colour of its settings, it is Lean's most intimate film since the early fifties: a sparse, tightly con-

(Left) Gandhi's funeral procession – a spectacular scene in a film of spectacular scenes. (Below left) Oscar winners Ben Kingsley as Gandhi and Richard Attenborough as Richard Attenborough.

trolled (if slightly slow) study of relationships, to which India, notwithstanding the expectations created by the current rage for Raj films, is basically just a background – a thematically crucial one, but a background nonetheless.

Doubtless, *A Passage to India* will be recruited into the ranks of the British film renaissance – but if the renaissance does have a father figure – or, to be more precise, an avuncular one – it is not Sir David Lean, but Sir Richard Attenborough, whose irrepressibly jovial-but-sincere presence has been on hand to fly the flag of British cinema at almost every juncture. Attenborough's readiness to seize every opportunity to promote British cinema has, over the past two or three years, done much to fuel the idea of a renaissance. *Gandhi*, which he cherished as an idea for over a decade and finally steered into production with the help of Goldcrest, won eight of the twelve major Oscars – an all-time record for a British film. Coming in the wake of *Chariots of Fire*'s pair of awards, *Gandhi*'s barrowful turned a trend into a reality. In Hollywood, a reaction may have set in – 1984 contenders like *Educating Rita* and *The Dresser*, and 1985's *A Passage to India* and *The Killing Fields* may well have left Los Angeles' Music Center empty-handed *because* they were British. But for the world at large, the renaissance remains a reality.

The postwar generation of film-makers have continued to work as they have always done, of course, though with very mixed results. John Schlesinger may have been the doyen of the last renaissance, but his 1981 comedy, *Honky Tonk Freeway,* was a $25 million disaster, and his two subsequent projects have been either small-scale – his TV film of Alan Bennett's play, *An Englishman Abroad* (1983) – or impersonal (the factually based 1985 thriller, *The Falcon and the Snowman.*) In any case, *Honky Tonk Freeway,* although British financed (it was one of a trio of films that led to a massive upheaval in Thorn EMI's production arm), was set in Florida; and *The Falcon and the Snowman,* despite the David Bowie theme song, 'This is not America', is a 100 per cent American movie. Other directors of the same generation who have left the British Isles for Hollywood include Ken Russell – whose American movies of the eighties consist of the preposterous psychedelic drama, *Altered States* (1980), and the equally appalling sexual melodrama, *Crimes of Passion* (1984) – and Tony Richardson, one of the leading figures of British film-making in the fifties and early sixties, who has been firmly settled in Hollywood since the failure of his attempt to re-do *Tom Jones* with *Joseph Andrews* in 1977. Richardson's two most recent Hollywood films, *The Border* (1981) and *The Hotel New Hampshire* (1984), have both been commercial failures. Quirky, well-intentioned but uneven, they seem to epitomize the problems of a British director treating American subjects in a 'British' style: *The Border* is a social drama, *Hotel New Hampshire* an offbeat comedy, but neither seems to have captured the imagination of the American public.

Another stalwart of the fifties renaissance, Lindsay Anderson, seemed equally off-form with his 1982 state-of-the-nation survey, *Britannia Hospital,* a supposedly classical satire of Britain in the style of Hogarth's cartoons, which flopped badly. Anderson has long been one of the most acerbic critics of other film-makers, film writers and reviewers, and there may have been a touch of glee in the way in which *Britannia Hospital* was rubbished by certain critics. But there can be no denying that the clearness of eye and readiness of wit which characterised Anderson's films like *If . . .* and *O Lucky Man* were conspicuously lacking in his 1982 film. More successful – though with greatly superior material – was Karel Reisz, with his screen version of *The French Lieutenant's Woman,* a 1981 prestige production that was oddly missing from the list of Oscar nominations. With an interesting script by Harold Pinter that tried to reproduce in filmic terms the

DEE DEE GLASS

Born in Chicago in 1948, Dee Dee Glass entered film-making via radical politics in the late sixties. Then, when she came to England in 1972, she found she had picked up a skill – editing videotape – which was very rare in those days. From a year's project editing tape at the National Film School, she went on to work as a researcher on Granada's *Crown Court,* moved to Southern Television as a director, then was instrumental in the setting up of Reality Productions, a film company, with Seona Robertson and Diane Tammes.

Reality was the production company for *Sacred Hearts,* directed by Barbara Rennie, shot in the summer of 1984, and premiered at the London Film Festival. Earlier, though, Glass had been part of Broadside, the all-woman television production company and the question of sexual politics in film remains of considerable importance to her. However this hadn't, she insists, been a prime consideration on *Sacred Hearts.*

'It wasn't until the Production Manager added it all up that I realised that, on most features, 20% of the crew are female and 80% male and we'd reversed it! So I think *part* of the interest is in that, but part of it also is in the way we actually work together, which is to do with our politics and with our being a co-operative. My going onto the set is not 'the producer' being on the set: for Diane and Barbara and the crew, I'm just somebody you can send off to get coffee. Which is actually very nice, because why the hell shouldn't I? I've got nothing else to do!'

Nor does she really aim for an all-woman crew in the future. 'I think that, in the past fifteen years or so, a fair number of men's attitudes towards life have been transformed by the women's movement, and those men are great to work with. What Diane and I *do* feel very strongly about, though, is encouraging women in technical areas: I actually think it's more important that there be more camerawomen and more women sparks and women sound recordists than women producers.'

complexities of John Fowles's novel, it strove hard to be more than a costume drama and generally succeeded.

Britain's other distinctive talents of the seventies have met with mixed fortunes in the eighties. Nicholas Roeg, having started the decade unpromisingly with *Bad Timing* (1980), came up in 1983 with one of his strangest and, to my thinking, greatest films, *Eureka*, a British-American co-production, produced by Jeremy Thomas, one of Britain's more adventurous young producers, which has a disastrous reception and was scarcely released in Britain. A story of sex, violence and gold which covers fifty years and the two extremities of the North American continent, *Eureka* is stunningly beautiful to look at and constantly challenging. Roeg has since made *Insignificance*, again produced by Thomas, a film version of the stage play which was unreleased at time of writing. John Boorman, a director of equal ambition – but who, with *Deliverance* (1972), had the big box office success that has always eluded Roeg – came up with a strange, compelling and distinctly anti-mythic treatment of the Arthurian legend in *Excalibur* (1981). Since then, he has produced *Dream One*, an adult fantasy shot in a bubble outside Paris, and has directed his South American epic, *The Emerald Forest* – a film whose production history has been distinctly chequered.

Finally, the team of Ken Loach and Tony Garnett, who did more than anyone else to revolutionize the methods of British television drama (and, by extension, the cinema) in the sixties, have both had films out as directors in the eighties, neither with much commercial success, and neither with the same evidence of energy and commitment that characterized their work together in previous decades. Loach's costume drama, *Black Jack* (made in 1979), hardly seemed in line with the rest of his work; his docudrama on the young umemployed, *Looks and Smiles* (1983), first shown on ITV, then given theatrical release, gave the impression of covering ground that Loach had covered better and more passionately before. Garnett's first film as a director, *Prostitute* (1980), on the other hand, was pretty much in keeping with the pair's earlier efforts, but his American-made feature, *Hand Gun* (1983), about sexism and the gun laws in the State of Texas, was an unhappy compromise with the dictates of commercial film-making which neither did justice to its subject not did well at the box office.

With the exception, then, of British cinema's

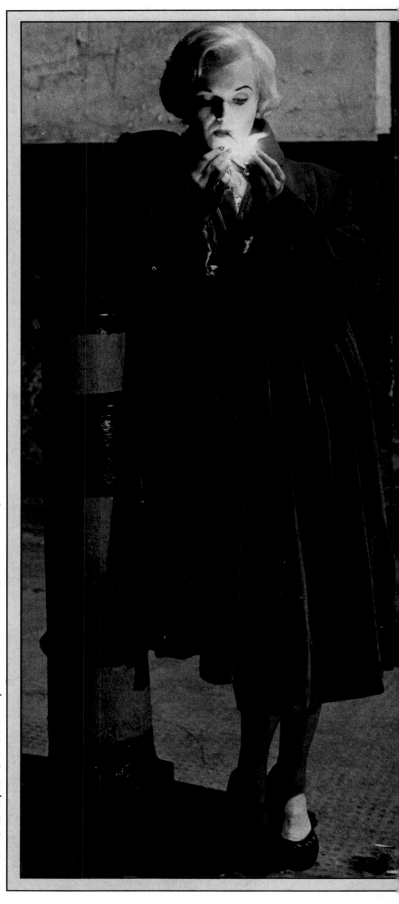

MAMOUN HASSAN

With Mamoun Hassan as its Managing Director, the National Film Finance Corporation took on a new lease of life, becoming an active and vital force in British film production, helping to make such films as *Gregory's Girl*, *Britannia Hospital*, *Another Country* and *Dance with a Stranger*. Not surprisingly, Hassan – whose background is as a film editor and a director of TV documentaries – was a little bitter about the government's decision to close down the NFFC.

'The Corporation still has a crucial role to play, for the market place is just not big enough when you're talking about very high risk investments, and anyway, it's a distorted market place. That is why conservative, socialist and social democrat governments right across Europe support their film industries.

'The miracle is – and the White Paper doesn't seem to understand this – that, with £1.5 million a year, the NFFC has had an enormous influence, for good or ill. The White Paper indulged in flannel by saying our record was good. Our record was a miracle – not just the films, but the role we played in the industry.

'Without the NFFC, the danger may not be apparant at the present, because the patient is actually alive and, considering his age, doing as well as can be expected. But the next time he is knocked down by the flu, I don't think he'll recover.'

Dance With a Stranger (1985).

senior members, Attenborough and Lean, the directors of the fifties seem to have been rather fazed by the methods and the subject matter of the eighties. The one director with a distinctive personal style, Tony Richardson, has been the one least able to bring it into line with the tone of the present decade. The cinema is, after all, a thing of the moment as well as a timeless art form, and survival in it requires either a chameleon-like quality or a strong personal trade mark.

The chameleon quality has generally served the British film industry well; it has survived best when it has simply serviced the needs of others. In the fifties, for instance, M-G-M flourished with its locally made Olde England swashbucklers like *Ivanhoe* and *Quentin Durward*. In the years since, American companies have rented British studio space and used British locations to make films which only ocassionally have the alibi of a British setting. By the same token, those directors who have stayed most consistently in work have been the ones who had the least difficulty in adapting to the needs of the market place. Like Hollywood in the thirties, the British cinema has had its contract directors – men whose chief skill has been an ability to deliver the goods, on time on budget. If film is indeed an industry before it is on art form, it needs its time-and-motion men. The British cinema has had some very good ones.

Former assistant director Guy Hamilton, for example, who was responsible for several of the early Bond films, has turned to another source of whodunnits in the eighties, directing two Agatha Christie tales – *The Mirror Crack'd* in 1981 and *Evil Under the Sun* in 1982 – with lots of cameo roles for guest stars. Taking over the Bond mantle from Hamilton (and a gaggle of other directors), former second unit director John Glen has helmed all the Bond films of the decade – *For Your Eyes Only* (1981), *Octopussy* (1983) and *A View to a Kill* (1985). The Bond movies now operate on a two-year cycle: the traditional June opening gives way almost immediately to pre-production on the next one, with scripting, planning and casting continuing into the following spring, when second unit work begins the stunts, the chases, the action sequences and the spectacular settings (for a *View to a Kill*, Iceland and Switzerland); principal photography ends around Christmas, with the last couple of months spent on the Pinewood lot; finally, the remainder of the winter and the spring are used up in pre-production and preparation for the June opening. As a result, Glen is in more or less permanent Bondage, and the result of that continuity of experience shows in the skill with which the telling of the tales is handled, even if the tales themselves have been getting rather thin of late.

Another Bond alumnus, Lewis Gilbert (he did the first of the really big Bond movies, *You Only Live Twice*, in 1967, and *The Spy Who Loved Me* in 1977) similarly came up from within the industry, and is likewise very much a professional director. Gilbert is no amateur, but he has brought to certain of his films a very definitive stamp, namely to handle unusual and/or unfortunate romantic or sexual relationships with sensitivity and skill. He showed it in *The Greengage Summer* (1961) and in *Alfie* (1966), and he confirmed it in the eighties with *Educating Rita* (1983), a solidly commercial (and solidly successful) treatment of Willy Russell's play about a working-class student (Julie Walters) who has an affair of sorts with her mildly alcoholic tutor (Michael Caine). As Caine, himself a consummate professional, puts it, 'without wishing this to sound in any way a criticism, Lewis is a workmanlike director'. Every national cinema needs its workmanlike directors, and Britain's is no exception.

Brief mention should also be made of other 'workmanlike' directors: John Irvin, who, after *The Dogs of War* (1980) and the disastrous *Ghost Story* in 1981, directed the far more successful *Champions* in 1984, and will soon release *Turtle Summer*, based on

Russell Hoban's charming, sad little novel about two middle-aged misfits who set free the giant turtles from London Zoo; Alan Bridges, whose film, *The Hireling,* won the Palme d'Or at Cannes in 1983, and who has made two rather pedestrian Edwardian period pieces in the eighties, *Return of the Soldier* (1982) and *The Shooting Party* (1984); Michael Winner, one of the British industry's most outspoken figures, who brought out some including the costume remake, *The Wicked Lady* in 1983; Richard Marquand who, after directing a tautly efficient thriller, *Eye of the Needle,* in 1981, got a shot at the blockbuster market in 1983, when he directed the third *Star Wars* film, *Return of the Jedi* and John Hough, who has made some distinctive horror movies including *Twins of Evil* (1971) and the *The Legend of Hell House* (1973, in the US), but who has not really found his feet in the eighties, during which he last directed the unsuccessful *Watcher in the Woods* for Disney in 1982, the Canadian horror movie, *Incubus,* in 1983, and the Spanish-made sequel to a sequel, *Triumphs of a Man Called Horse* (1984).

For many of the above-named directors, television has been both a training ground and a source of work between features: although a Hollywood director can expect to work almost full-time for the big screen, a British one is likely to have to turn his or her hand to a number of other forms of film-making – commercials, television drama, tele-vision series – in order to make a living. Certainly, television money – from Channel 4 – has been behind much of the present renaissance. And the directors of some of the most distinctive films of the eighties have come from (and gone back to) tele-vision. Jack Gold's career for instance (with such work as the Quentin Crisp 'biography', *The Naked Civil Servant*), has been far more successful than his big screen efforts, but his just-completed theatrical feature, *Street Dreams,* may shift the balance.

Strangely enough, one of the British 'renaissance' films that has made the biggest mark in the United States, Peter Duffell's *Experience Preferred, But Not Essential,* has been seen only on TV in Britain. A slight, nostalgic story about a girl taking a holiday job in a hotel in a Welsh coastal resort during the fifties, it is brought to life by Duffell's sensitive direction of the young performers. Even Duffell, however, could make little of *The Far Pavilions,* the most outrageous of the India cycle films, again shown theatrically abroad and on television in Britain. With a largely Caucasian cast made up to look like Indians, this interminable version of M. M. Kaye's Mills & Boon romance of the North-west Frontier is watchable only for its Indian landscape, its settings and its elephants: the people and the performances all belong in purdah.

The two most notable TV directors to make their mark on British cinema in the eighties, however, have been Stephen Frears and Dick Clement.

(Opposite, top) Judi Bowker as Lady Olivia in Alan Bridges' exquisitely mounted *The Shooting Party* (1985). (Opposite, bottom) James Mason as Sir Randolph Nettleby in *The Shooting Party,* the last film of his distinguished career. (Left) Julie Walters as the eponymous heroine, Michael Caine as her alcoholic tutor in Lewis Gilbert's *Educating Rita* (1983).

Frears, a veteran of many TV plays, returned to the cinema in 1984 for the first time since *Gumshoe* in 1971 (though his 1979 TV film, *Bloody Kids*, did get a theatrical release in 1984) to make *The Hit*, an oddball thriller that follows John Hurt, Terence Stamp, Tim Roth and *Carmen*'s Laura del Sol across Spain in a spare, stylish chase, where what happens is consistently less important than the way in which it happens, and even than what doesn't happen. Dick Clement, who, with Ian Le Fresnais, wrote such TV classics as *The Likely Lads*, *Porridge* and *Auf Wiedersehen, Pet*, has played it fairly safe in his debut features as director. His first, made by HandMade Films, was the slightly awkward but likeable adventure spoof, *Bullshot* (1983). His next film was *Water* (1985), also a HandMade film, and one of the best mainstream comedies to come out of the British cinema in a decade. Set on a Carribean Island called Cascara, *Water* courts disaster in its subject matter – a singing mulatto revolutionary played by Scottish comedian Billy Connolly, a pot-smoking Governor (Michael Caine) with a nympho-maniac wife (Brenda Vaccaro), and a string of other characters and situations from the bad old days of British music hall – but somehow manages to emerge as a funny, tightly paced and highly enjoy-able comedy, pushing the British film renaissance into an area in which, with the exception of the films of Bill Forsyth, it has not been notably successful.

The British film renaissance, though, belongs not to the mechanics, nor to the TV moonlighters, but two quite distinct groups of directors: those who in previous decades successfully combined a personal style of film-making with commercial success and continued to do so in the eighties; and those who found the chance to make their first, more personal features in the improved climate of the eighties. Of the former – Britain's Hollywood auteurs, who went West in geographical terms only – some have stayed put on the far side of the pond, keeping their British passports but making American movies.

(Above) Ron House, Alan Shearman and Diz White in *Bullshot!* (Below left) Billy Connolly and Michael Caine in *Water*. (Right) Ian Le Frenais and Dick Clement (producer and director) on the set of *Water*.

MICHAEL WHITE

Michael White is basically a theatrical entrepreneur, with something of a reputation for the parties he gives. But he has also been pretty active in the film industry, producing such films as *The Rocky Horror Picture Show*, *Jabberwockey*, *Rude Boy*, *Shock Treatment*, *Polyester*, *My Dinner with André* and the forthcoming Comic Strip film, *The Supergrass*. And, having struggled more than most people to put the money packages together, he is more outspoken about the situation than most.

'It's tragic – tragic isn't too strong a word for it – about the financing of British films in relation to other British industries. Let's take a figure at random: if you'd put 3% of what's gone into the motor industry, we'd be singing!

'There's no way out of this, as long as politicians on both sides of the House of Commons are so totally disinterested in the arts. They pay lip service, they go to the opening of the Barbican or the Royal Variety Show or the Royal Film Premiere. But people who are politically-minded in this country, with very few exceptions, feel that the arts are something that are a bit of a waste of time.

'If the first Wilson Government had said, alright, let's put £100 million down for the next ten years for the film industry, not only would they have made two billion or whatever out of it, but they would also have had a terrific ride for their money.

'Look at Australia: it's been incredibly beneficial for them. They're big news. They've hit the consciousness of people who aren't even interested. Everybody who's semi-literate now knows that Australia has a thriving film industry and makes good films and is an interesting place. We could have had that.'

Adrian Lyne, a graduate of TV commercials, made an impressive dent in the awful predictability of American teenage sex dramas with the surprisingly compulsive *Foxes* in 1979. In 1983, he hit the big time in the same area with *Flashdance*. More recently, Lyne has tackled explicit sexual relationships in *9½ Weeks*, which explores the characters and the bodies of Kim Basinger and Mickey Rourke. Roger Spottiswoode, having been brought in to rescue the formulary disaster movie, *Terror Train*, has gone on to make one of America's most skilful political dramas of the eighties, *Under Fire* (1983), and Ridley Scott, another graduate of the world of commercials (he did the famous Hovis ads), made his 'art movie' in 1977 – *The Duellists*, produced by David Puttnam – then settled for being master of the thinking person's sci-fi epic. After making *Alien* (1979) in Britain he made *Blade Runner* (1982), an American megaproduction which tried to graft Raymond Chandler onto science fiction novelist, Philip K. Dick (and flopped badly at the box office), and is currently directing *Legend*, another large-scale futuristic enterprise, at Pinewood.

Four British directors, however, have kept particularly active in the cinematic mainstream during the eighties: Michael Apted, Hugh Hudson, Alan Parker and Peter Yates. Of the four, only Apted has made all his features in the United States, and only Hudson all his in Britain; Parker and Yates have flitted back and forth between the two.

Apted, long thought of as one of the industry's contract directors, is in fact a film-maker of considerable skill and sensitivity, though he explicitly rejects the label of an auteur. Perhaps it is his suburban upbringing (in Ilford, Essex) that has given him his greatest attribute: an ability to develop a strong sense of place in his films. Like many who come from a neutral background, he has been able to recognise and reproduce those elements in strongly characterised backgrounds which make them memorable – a process he started when he moved north to work on the Manchester-based soap opera, *Coronation Street*, for Granada Television.

Apted's *Coalminer's Daughter* (1980), which won a Best Actress award for Sissy Spacek, is an extraordinary achievement for a foreigner – a portrait of the Kentucky-born country singer, Loretta Lynn. Less successful – though underrated in Britain – was Apted's follow-up, the John Belushi film *Continental Divide* (1981), which sends a chain-smoking, overweight Chicago newsman (Belushi) off into the wilds of the Rockies and manages to create a romance out

HUGH HUDSON

Hugh Hudson is a successful director of television commercials, who entered features comparatively late – though he had previously gone outside the thirty-second format with a number of sponsored documentaries – when he directed *Chariots of Fire* (1981). The rest, as they say, is history.

Chariots seemed to make Hudson a spokesman for the new 'Britishness' – British films that quietly but effectively celebrated the re-emerging national consciousness. And his second feature, *Greystoke – The Legend of Tarzan, Lord of the Apes* (1984) rather confirmed the feeling. But Hudson is now working on *Revolution* – about America in 1776 – and turns out to be fairly off-hand on the question of cinematic nationality.

'*Greystoke* is an American film – a Warners project from the very start – and Tarzan is an American hero, even if he is British by birth. In general, though, I don't mind where I work: I will go anywhere that the story tells me to go. Where the money comes from is immaterial, as far as I am concerned. To want to have British money to make a 'British' film is neither here nor there.

'The world shouldn't be considered in terms of boundaries, especially in relation to creative work. Everything else is internationalized and, while there is an argument that says that is a shame, it is a fact of modern life.'

Hudson is also realistic about the director's right to final cut in the world of modern filmmaking. 'If you have a budget of more than $20 million, you are never going to have complete control of anything: you have to work in France for that. But I think Michaelangelo probably provided us with the best example here. He let the Pope go up the ladder for an occasional look, and he would talk about various things with him in the corner. But he would also splash a bit of paint on him, so he wouldn't want to come up too often.'

(Right) Director Hugh Hudson on the set of *Greystoke – The Legend of Tarzan, Lord of the Apes* (1984).

*Greystoke – The Legend of
Tarzan, Lord of the Apes,*
directed by **Hugh Hudson.**

of it. And *Gorky Park* (1983), a faithful adaptation of Martin Cruz Smith's Moscow-set thriller, impressively recreates the tone of the novel, even though Helsinki had to be substituted for Moscow during the shooting. In between *Continental Divide* and *Gorky Park*, Apted made a TV movie in the 'First Love' series for David Puttnam, *P'Tang Yang Kipperbang*, which, as plain *Kipperbang*, did quite well theatrically in the United States. There, though, a sense of place – the British provinces during the fifties – cannot really compensate for the inconclusiveness of Jack Rosenthal's script, even if the film did allow Apted to deal with one of his great loves, cricket (as a schoolboy, he used to open for the under-elevens with future English test captain, Mike Brierley).

Hugh Hudson, also a graduate of the commercials world, shot into the Oscar spotlight with his first feature, *Chariots of Fire* (though it was the film, not Hudson, that won the award). The film is characterised by a string of clearly signposted visual landmarks linked by a strong sense of emotional pacing – two things which it is not hard to trace back to the world of commercials. The combination has made the film especially easy to anthologize – the run on the beach at Broadstairs, the race round the quad at Caius, the Highland Games, the restaurant scene between Ben Cross and Alice Krige, the climactic 1924 Olympics in Paris – with each scene bathed in a sense of heroic nostalgia. To his subsequent film, *Greystroke – The Legend of Tarzan, Lord of the Apes* (1984), Hudson brought the same skills, turning the tale of the jungle lad who is brought back to his Edwardian family in Britain into a slightly contradictory celebration of both the charms of Edwardian civilisation and the joys of primitive existence. Beset by post-production problems, *Greystoke* had nothing like the impact of *Chariots*, but did well enough at the box office.

MICHAEL APTED

Michael Apted came into filmmaking from television, having worked on such Granada programmes as *World in Action* and *Coronation Street*. His first feature was *Triple Echo* (1972), and he made three more in Britain: *Stardust* (1974), *The Squeeze* (1977) and *Agatha* (1978). A fourth, the ill-fated *Trick or Treat* (1975), collapsed under him and never reached the screen.

At the end of the decade, Apted went to the United States to make *Coal Miner's Daughter* (1980). And, since then, his films have been American films – *Continental Divide* (1981) and *Gorky Park* (1983). He lives in Britain but his only British film of the eighties has been for television: the 'First Love' story, *P'Tang Yang Kipperbang* (1983).

Michael Apted is, he happily admits, a director of other people's ideas. 'A lot of directors make serious mistakes thinking of themselves as auteurs – a lot of very good directors. But the directors I most admire were very much people who were not *auteurs*, who were products of the studio system. And, in a way, I regard myself as a product of the English studio system: the television system. We worked in exactly the same way, all of us, whether we were Ken Loach or John Mackenzie or Jack Gold: we all did four or five things a year, because that's the way it was.

'I think it can be both a strength and a weakness, but I'm happy doing that: it's the *only* thing I can do. I can't write: I can work well with writers, but I am not an author. I would like to think that a fair bit of myself was in some of the material I chose. But I have to acknowledge that my strengths, since the very beginning at Granada, have been in researching stuff, finding stuff out, whether it was doing a *World in Action*, a play in Manchester, or a movie in Kentucky. That's me: that's what I do best.'

Older than Apted or Hudson, Peter Yates has been making films in Hollywood since *Bullitt* (1968). Recently, however, his films have been British-based, including the unsuccessful fairytale, *Krull* (1983), and the forthcoming version of Nicholas Cage's autobiographical novel, *Eleni* and *The Dresser* (1983), which belongs firmly in the renaissance bracket, given its multiple nominations at last year's Oscar ceremonies. Deprived of the action scenes into which he has always been able to breathe the real life of the picture, Yates does an honest if somewhat pedestrian job with *The Dresser*, though he does provide the opportunity for Albert Finney and Tom Courtenay to do some of their best (if scarcely most restrained) work.

Restraint is not a word generally associated with the last of the group, Alan Parker, who also entered feature films via TV commercials. In the eighties, three of Parker's four films have been American; *Fame* (1980), the energetic, streetwise musical which spawned a flaccid, suburban TV series; *Shoot the Moon* (1981), a far more personal film about a marriage cracking up, set among the supposedly self-aware owners of tennis courts and jacuzzis in California's Marin Country; and *Birdy* (1985), his strange and compulsive study of a mentally disturbed Vietnam veteran. Parker's other film, however – *Pink Floyd The Wall* (1982) – is very much a British one, taking the rock group's music as the basis for a kind of post-punk odyssey by its central character, Pink (Bob Geldof). An ambitious, sumptuous if finally flawed movie, *The Wall* shows Parker beyond the mere images and the realist surfaces that have characterised British cinema. Though not an unqualified success, it represents the sort of ambitions and experiments that mainstream British cinema needs.

(Opposite page) Alan Parker's *Birdy* (1985). (Below) *Shoot the Moon* (1981). (This page) Albert Finney as Lear in *The Dresser*, directed by Peter Yates. (Below) Peter Yate's unsuccessful sci-fi fairytale *Krull* (1983).

TERRY GILLIAM

Terry Gilliam's road to directing features is different from that of most of the other directors in this book. Born in Minneapolis, raised in Los Angeles, he is a comics enthusiast who first came to London as an illustrator. Having acquired a certain reputation, he started doing the montages for the TV series, *Monty Python's Flying Circus*.

When the Pythons went into pictures, so did Gilliam. He co-directed *Monty Python and the Holy Grail* (1975), then went solo with *Jabberwocky* (1976) – which, he insists, is *not* a Python film – and broke free from the group more decisively with *Time Bandits* (1980).

The methods he used as an illustrator have served him well in the movies, both on *Jabberwocky* and *Time Bandits*, and on this year's $14-million serio-comic fantasy, *Brazil*. 'With *Jabberwocky*, I did enormous amounts of research: I really just steeped myself in medieval material, then I threw it all away and winged it. If an idea came up that seemed right, I went with it. And then, what was interesting, after we'd finished the film, was that I kept discovering specific things that we'd done that had just seemed like a good idea, and that were absolutely accurate!

'It's that thing of being absorbed enough by the film that it's running you. *Brazil* ran me. I got very mystical about it: *somebody* was making the film, and it wasn't me! It was like in *Time Bandits:* I just tried to be a kid again, totally. I thought and tried to live like a twelve-year-old kid. I do what an actor does: I get into it, so that any decision I make, it's the twelve-year-old making the decision.'

(Above) **Bob Hoskins as Harold Shand, London's top racketeer about to experience a** *Long Good Friday*. **(Below) Michael Palin (Charles Fortescue) and Michael Hordern (Slatterthwaite) in** *The Missionary*. **(Right) the two faces of Jonathan Pryce in Terry Gilliam's** *Brazil* **(1985).**

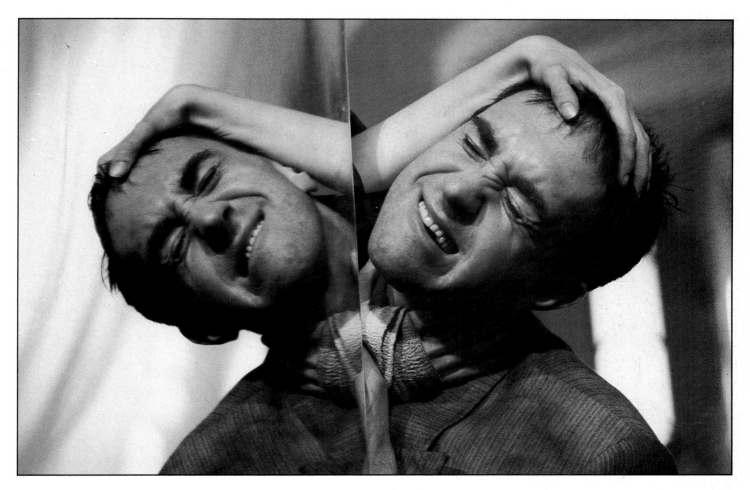

The renaissance proper has really been fuelled by newer, less immediately accessible – and less commercial – talents, generally aged between thirty and forty. Not that all the new British directors of that age necessarily belong in the same category. Some, like former TV director Richard Loncraine (*Brimstone and Treacle*, 1982, and *The Missionary*, 1983), have simply found a niche within smaller-scale commercial film-making. Others, like Terry Gilliam, the American who did the montages for *Monty Python's Flying Circus*, have used the leverage to make their own quirkily commercial films – like *Time Bandits* (1980) and *Brazil* (1985), comedies which grew less obviously comic and more evidently personal. John Mackenzie, with extensive TV experience, was behind the best British thriller in a decade, *The Long Good Friday* (1981), then progressed to the efficient but rather characterless Graham Greene tale, *The Honorary Consul* (1983). Julien Temple, after the memorable Sex Pistols film, *The Great Rock 'n Roll Swindle* (1980), turned his attention to pop videos (he made the partly banned Rolling Stones 'Under Cover' video), and is only now coming back into feature film-making again, with the forthcoming *Absolute Beginners*, part-

produced by Virgin Films, the company originally brought into existence to distribute *The Great Rock 'n Roll Swindle*.

Other names belong to the renaissance, too: Charles Sturridge, who directed most of the massive television adaptation of Evelyn Waugh's *Brideshead Revisited*, and who has so far made one feature, the disappointing *Runners* (1983), about children who run away from home; Marek Kanievska, one of the directors of the *Shoestring* TV series, who made a consummate hit out of the film version of *Another Country* (1984); Roland Joffé, veteran of TV plays like *Spongers* and *United Kingdom*, who ended up with an Oscar nomination for his first feature, *The Killing Fields*, about the war in Cambodia; Film School graduate Malcolm Mowbray, who produced the surprise success of last winter, *A Private Function*, a nostalgic comedy from an Alan Bennett script about a chiropodist (Michael Palin) in a small Yorkshire town who becomes embroiled in a plot to save a pig called Betty for the black-market dinner table; emigré Brit Alex Cox, who made *Repo Man* (1984), one of last year's best American films; and Steve Barron, one of the most innovative of Britain's pop video makers, who launched into features in

STEVE BARRON

With a string of award-winning videos behind him – for British groups like Heaven 17 and The Human League, and superstars like Phil Collins and Michael Jackson (for whom he made the 'Billie Jean' video), Steve Barron was one of the veterans of the pop video industry by the time he was 26. He also came from a film industry background: his mother, continuity person Zelda Barron, who directed *Secret Places*, has been in the business for twenty years, and Steve himself has worked his way up from clapper-loader to cameraman to director.

Rusty Lemorande, producer of *Electric Dreams*, first saw Steve's videos when his mum took them on to the *Yentl* set (Lemorande was producing, Barron was doing continuity). Then Lemorande gave her a script to read from a technician's point of view, and she passed it on to her son . . .

'After Billie Jean,' says Steve, 'I started getting offers of all kinds – quite a few scripts and things. It became a channel I was going down, although I told everyone I didn't want to do features. And then *Electric Dreams* came along.

'I wouldn't have learned about shooting and cutting without rock videos. It was purely a question of, Let's try this. I still don't know how it works: I just know from reaction. You do something and people like it, you do something else and people like it, and when you come along to do your third thing, you can choose one of the two options of the way you went before.

'Videos and features are the same to a certain extent, you are working commercially, for what people want. It is obviously transition too, though, dealing with actors and the whole dramatic side of things is something you never deal with in video. But I couldn't have done it without the videos.'

(Above) **Roland Joffé on the set of *The Killing Fields* (1984) with Dr. Haing S. Ngor (Dith Pran) and Sam Waterston (Sydney Schanberg). (Below) Anna Massey and Rupert Everett in Marek Kanievska's *Another Country* (1984).**

1984 with the ill-fated *Electric Dreams*, a tale of romance and computers in contemporary San Francisco, which showed a narrative skill and a sense of tone that suggested his move from videos to features was a natural one.

TONY SMITH

Since Tony Smith took over as Director of the British Film Institute, the BFI's public image has been transformed, from a respectable keeper of information to something with a higher profile. Success with films like *The Draughtsman's Contract* and *Ascendancy* has obviously helped. But, believes Smith, those successes are all part of a wider game plan.

'I don't think it's just an Act of God: I think that what the BFI has been doing, what Channel 4 has been doing, the kind of programming that other television organisations are now moving to, is the result of hard work. Some of us are seeing the result of things we've worked for for years and years.

'What the BFI Production Board does is make a series of interventions into the processes and artistic approaches of British film-making. If you look at the script of *The Draughtsman's Contract*, you'll see it's non-commercial: even now, after it's made a lot of money, it's *still* non-commercial. And yet, we have made it possible for the film-maker concerned to make his next film without public money.

'And that's what we're trying to do: we're trying to construct film-makers. They're very complicated things to make. The nearest thing in the academic world are nuclear physicists and brain surgeons. Between the medical school and the ability to be a brain surgeon, a wide variety of experiments and training has to come. And, in the case of the film industry, there's nowhere to do it – nowhere between that pure, educative stage and being fully commercial. We try to supply that.'

£2 for parking –
£5 for tickets –
£2.50 for drinks – all to see a dopey great twit in blue tights and a cape, prance around in the sky...

Alan Parker

But it is the work of half a dozen directors that has given the renaissance its real tone, and which, with their varying concerns and achievements, have seemed to offer the most for the future. Ed Bennett, whose film, *Ascendancy*, won the Golden Bear at Berlin in 1983, has, like James Scott, come out of the tradition of alternative cinema (his previous films have been documentaries of, more properly, film essays, like 1980's *Four Questions About Art*). *Ascendancy* owes much to this background in terms of subject matter – the historical background to the present situation in Northern Ireland. But its treatment is closer to the world of the TV play: a narrative viewed from the standpoint of the semi-catatonic daughter (Julie Covington) of a Belfast businessman. It is a brave film rather than a successful one, trying hard to combine radical content with an accessible form, and trying equally hard to bring some fresh light to bear on the murderous conflicts of Ulster. In both respects, it is partly successful.

In terms of commercial success, Chris Petit's films have been even more marginal, with only his first feature, *Radio On* (1979), getting any real distribution in the UK. Petit, former films editor of *Time Out* magazine, is perhaps the only one of the current crop of film-makers to belong to a European – as opposed to an American or television – tradition. With a reputation as an often acerbic critic of British cinema, he has not exactly received a friendly welcome from the British film industry. His 1982 film, *An Unsuitable Job for a Woman*, based on one of P. D. James's thrillers, suffered from any number of compromises – budget cutbacks, filming in the Home Counties rather than on the Cambridgeshire fens so essential to James's stories. It was ultimately an unsatisfactory work, though partially redeemed by Petit's skill at framing relationships (visually and contextually) and by the quality of the cinematography by Martin Schafer (Wim Wenders's cameraman), which manages to make the familiar look strange.

Petit's next feature, *Flight to Berlin* (1984), was backed by the BFI Production Board (as were Bennett's *Ascendancy* and Greenway's *The Draughtsman's Contract*), with additional finance from West Germany. It is one of the most *different* films to come out of the renaissance – thriller in the tradition of Jean-Luc Godard, which manages to turn the search for clues and information into a strange, metaphysical quest. Though originally planned for Paris and switched to Berlin for financial reasons, its tone is ideally suited to that city's bleakness and claustrophobia.

Different, too, is Neil Jordan, an Irish novelist who worked as 'creative consultant' on John Boorman's *Excalibur*, before Boorman returned the compliment by helping him with his notable debut as a feature director, *Angel* (1982), a TV film that had wide theatrical release. I have felt that both *Angel* and Jordan's much more successful second feature, *Company of Wolves* (1984), were massively overrated – the work of someone with a strong visual imagination, but little dramatic or, for that matter, cinematic instinct. But I should record that Jordan has been hailed as the first film poet of the renaissance, capable of turning the present reality of Northern Ireland into an existential dreamworld in *Angel*, and of creating a full-blown sexual fantasy with *Company of Wolves*, the story of a young girl in an eerie forest and her final (presumed) acceptance of carnality. Given the absence of poetry from British cinema, I would like to be able to hail Jordan's films. Anyway, I appear to be in a minority.

Of Richard Eyre, a theatre and TV director who came to features in 1983 with *The Ploughman's Lunch*, not even his greatest admirers are likely to use the term 'poet'. In that film, Eyre produced, from Ian McEwan's script (the pair had already done *The Imitation Game* for television), a cold, unloving and unlovely portrait of a modern Briton, BBC newsman James Penfold (Jonathan Pryce). The film's failing is McEwan's, not Eyre's: with no centre, it becomes a work of deftly executed surface sketches. Made for Channel 4, it had perhaps the widest theatrical exposure of that first batch of TV movies. In the year following it Eyre directed two more features: *Loose Connections*, written by Maggie Brooks, a film school graduate scripting her first feature; and *Laughterhouse*, a comedy about driving a flock of geese to London which has improbable echoes of Howard Hawks's *Red River*, and a script by actor Brian Glover. Both show signs of having been rushed into production – a symptom of film renaissances everywhere – but from a directorial point of view, both have enough qualities to rescue them from the oblivion into which uninspired promotional and release patterns have consigned them. The truth is that Eyre has yet to find a big-screen subject which really suits him.

Two remaining newcomers represent by far the best hopes for the reviving British film industry. Michael Radford and Bill Forsyth have been friends since meeting at the Film School (Radford stayed the course, Forsyth didn't), and have, between them, directed half a dozen of the most interesting British films of the past ten years. Radford's first feature, *Another Time, Another Place* (1983), had that crucial feel of something *new* happening on the screen – a spark that has glimmered only fitfully in the British film renaissance. The story of a group of Italian prisoners of war on a remote Scottish farm during World War II, it has an authenticity of feeling and an intensity of emotion which is extremely rare in the British cinema.

Even more compulsive – though arguably not quite as good – is the film Radford followed it up with, a version of George Orwell's *1984* (1984) that exactly captured the depression bleakness and stasis of Orwell's novel. Unlike *Another Time, Another Place,* which was made with television money (Rediffusion and Channel 4), *1984* was an entirely commercial undertaking, and resulted in some acrimony when the film's producer (Simon Perry) and Radford accused the financing company, Virgin, of imposing on them a soundtrack by the Eurythmics (which did nothing to dent the film's box office success).

MICHAEL RADFORD

A Film School graduate who spent a good few years making films for the Central Office of Information and doing plays for the BBC, Michael Radford first came to the fore in the world of the big screen when his film, *Another Time, Another Place,* was selected for the Directors' Fortnight at Cannes in 1983.

Since then, he has gone on to much bigger things, directing the film of George Orwell's *1984,* for which he also wrote the script, and which starred John Hurt and Richard Burton in his last screen role. Enormously successful at the box office, *1984* won Best Film at last year's Standard Film Awards.

But his beginnings, and the way he came to be accepted at the Film School – after university and a brief spell as an actor – should be reassuring for newcomers. 'I was teaching Liberal Studies to gas fitters and plumbers at a college in Edinburgh, and I found a film camera. So, we improvised a movie on 16mm, silent. I knew nothing about film at all; and, even though it was silent, we built

a clapperboard and were told to solemnly clap on every shot. Then we sent all this silent stuff off to Kodak to be processed!

'It was a great initiation, though, because it was reversal stock and I was cutting with a glue splicer: every cut you made was *it!* I sent it off to the Film School, which was just starting and was being heavily publicized and they accepted me!

'We had this wonderful meeting at the National Film Theatre. We were all there, and Colin Young (Director of the NFTS) stood up – it's engraved in my memory, because it represented a complete change of life for me, and was very important – and said: "I'm just going to read out the list of films, and I want you to say whether your film is Com Mag, Com Opt or Sep Mag". I didn't know what he was talking about! Then he got to R, and he said, 'Radford: Oh, yes: yours is a silent film', and moved on. I breathed a sigh of relief, because I thought that, at any moment, my whole life was going to collapse in ruins!'

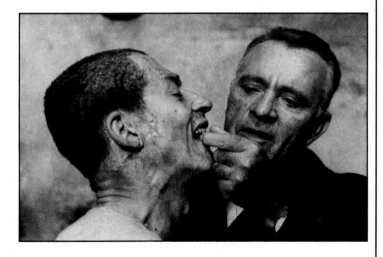

(Left) Neil Jordan's
Company of Wolves (1984).
(Above) John Hurt and
Richard Burton in Michael
Radford's *1984.*

It is the films of Bill Forsyth, however, which have provided many of the brightest moment of the renaissance. From *That Sinking Feeling* (1979) through *Gregory's Girl* (1980), *Local Hero* (1983) and *Comfort and Joy* (1984), they have shown the development of a film-maker of unique talent, able to observe the behaviour of real people, then turn that behaviour into the heightened reality of a dramatic story. His Gregory (Gordon John Sinclair), a gangling misfit of a Glasgow teenager, encapsulates the dreams and disappointments of adolescence without ever romanticizing them; and the film is that very rare thing among comedies of teenage love – a funny film that isn't cute. *Local Hero*, produced by David Puttnam with an international cast headed by Burt Lancaster, is a less sure-footed exercise. The story of a Scottish fishing village that is threatened by takeover from a Texas oil company, its initial avoidance of the cliches of Tartanry – that bane of postwar films about Scotland – does not really carry through to the end. An always entertaining film, *Local Hero* is, to me, a disappointment in Forsyth's career.

Not so *Comfort and Joy*, the only one of the current crop I have been inclined to include in my top ten British films of all time. A film which was coolly received by the critics and given a disastrous release by Thorn EMI, it tells the story of a Glaswegian DJ (Bill Paterson) who loses his girl and spends the days of comfort and joy preceding Christmas in a miserable daze, moving gradually nearer the centre of a bizarre war between the city's ice cream vans. *Comfort and Joy* is both the funniest and the saddest film of the eighties – funny because of Forsyth's unerring eye for the oddities and exaggerations of human behaviour; sad because, unlike the heroes of previous Forsyth films, *Comfort and Joy*'s Dickie Bird has – and is offered – no protection against the unpleasantnesses of the world. A film which, because of its depth and detail, repays multiple viewings, it is the movie with which the British film renaissance came of age.

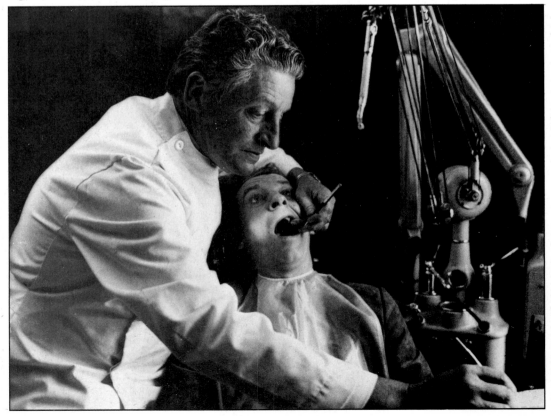

DAVID HARE

Vanessa Redgrave is Jean Travers in David Hare's *Wetherby* (1985).
(Top left) *Local Hero* and (below) *Comfort and Joy* from Bill Forsyth.

One of the leading British playwrights of the sixties and seventies, David Hare has described himself as 'a poet who needs a megaphone', whether it be theatre, television or films. And he has been successful in most areas: his plays, like *Fanshen* and *Plenty,* have become modern classics; his television dramas such as *Licking Hitler* and *Saigon: Year of the Cat,* have been highlights of British television. And, in 1985, his first cinema film, *Wetherby,* shared the Golden Bear at the Berlin Film Festival.

To make it, however, it was important for Hare to be working in the right context. And so, with other film makers, he set up a company called Greenpoint Films. 'We formed this company, Richard Eyre, Stephen Frears, John Mackenzie, Christopher Morahan, Simon Relph, Ann Scott and I, with the idea that we would be able to make films in the way we wanted, and with a minimum of interference. And also to be able to make the so-called 'difficult' projects.

'The thing is, it's very difficult to write uncommissioned screenplays: it involves a loss of confidence. Any other way, though, you're putting a year of your life aside for something which, if you're paid in advance, you're almost certainly going to have to compromise on. So, Greenpoint was a way of being able to write screenplays uncommissioned, and to see them through on my own terms.'

For most people, cinema is the 'big' art form, TV the small one. Hare sees it rather differently. 'My experience of television is that it has an extraordinary reach. I think *Saigon* played to something like 12½ million people, so you know you're reaching this enormous cross-section. And if you, so to speak, retreat back into the cinema to make films, then you're accepting that you're playing to a much smaller audience. But you're going to play to them under artistically much more satisfying conditions.'

Looking back over the films and film-makers discussed above, it is hard to discern any real thematic trends; there are at least as many themes as there are film-makers (and given the tendency of many British film-makers, raised in the world of the television play, to defer to the screenplay, probably more). But it is not hard to say what there has *not* been much of: costume drama, literary adaptations and genre pieces. Because British television has already got the field covered, from *Brideshead Revisited* to the BBC's Sunday afternoon Dickens adaptations, the British film renaissance has not felt the need, as have other emerging or re-emerging national cinemas, to explore the country's past and the origins of the present national identity. And, with the influence of Hollywood always hovering, British film-makers – with rare exceptions like *The Long Good Friday* and *The Hit* – have not indulged in generic exercises: crime thrillers have generally been restricted to television, horror movies have not been part of the British scene since Hammer in the sixties, and musicals have never found much place on the big screen in Britain.

What has been found in most of the films, however, is something which ought to characterise all contemporary drama: a tendency to go beyond the immediate characters of a story to present a portrait of a whole society. Obviously, *The Ploughman's Lunch*, with its closing scenes at the post-Falklands Conservative Party conference in Brighton, is the most obvious example. But all the films have elements of this about them – a legacy, perhaps, of the tendencies of British television drama and the atmosphere of the sixties in Britain, during which most of the present generation of film-makers were students. At all events, anatomies of Britain have abounded.

What really ties the present renaissance together, however, is not themes; it is money – for what has changed in the British film world of the eighties is the role of the producer. Instead of being just money raisers and controllers, producers have shared with directors a commitment to the kinds of film being made, and have set about finding new sources of money with which to do so. In addition to Puttnam and Jeremy Thomas, producers like Clive Parsons (*Gregory's Girl, Comfort and Joy*), Simon Perry (*Another Time, Another Place, Loose Connections* and *1984*) and Simon Ralph (*Return of the Soldier, The Ploughman's Lunch* and *Wetherby*, the outstanding film by David Hare which won the Golden Bear at the 1985 Berlin Film Festival) are as much a part of the renaissance as the film directors.

New supplies of money have been made available by a set of regulations introduced by the government at the turn of the decade (under the uninspiring name of Inland Revenue Statement of Practice SP9/79) and by the setting up of Channel 4. The exact terms of SP9/79 are complicated, but what it has meant is that *all* money invested in film production could be written off against tax in the first year, making it attractive for corporations with large tax bills to place money in film. The Channel 4 system is a lot simpler: it has provided up-front money for film production.

This situation is changing, however. The capital allowances scheme is now being phased out, and the Channel 4 honeymoon seems to be over. What is to be hoped is that, between them, they have set the ball rolling. Certainly, they have encouraged the establishment of production companies such as Goldcrest Films and Television, which recently announced a $60-million slate of feature films (even in Britain, film companies speak in dollars); Palace Pictures (*The Company of Wolves*), and a host of smaller ones. A flow of money has been set in motion, and it is this, perhaps, which provides the best hope for the continuation of the British film renaissance. Without money, there are no films.

The problems faced by the film industry in Britain do not really need to be rehearsed yet again: a small country with a population of, at best, recalcitrant cinemagoers, dominated by Hollywood and with a television tradition that takes away the need for a cinema culture (and receives Government protection in so doing). British film, if it is to go beyond the tenuous gains of the past four years' renaissance, needs a degree of support and help – from its potential audience, from its financial institutions, and above all from its legislators. The past four years have shown that we have the film-makers and that there is not, as François Truffaut once said, a contradiction between the words 'cinema' and 'British'. But the renaissance of the eighties has been the product of a set of circumstances which cannot be guaranteed to continue (indeed, several of them have ceased to exist already). Perhaps the momentum of what has been achieved as a result of those circumstances can be maintained. But nothing about the movie business is guaranteed, and that least of all.

AWARDS WON BY BRITISH FILMS

1980 Oscars –

BAFTA Best Costume Design: Shirley Russell (*Yanks*)
Best Supporting Actress: Rachel Roberts (*Yanks*)

Berlin –

Cannes Best Short Film: *Seaside Woman*

1981 Oscars Best Cinematography: Geoffrey Unsworth (*Tess*) (shared)
Best Costume Design: Anthony Powell (*Tess*)
Best Live-Action Short: *The Dollar Bottom*

BAFTA Best Actor: John Hurt (*The Elephant Man*)

Berlin –

Cannes Best Supporting Actor: Ian Holm (*Chariots of Fire*)

1982 Oscars Best Film: *Chariots of Fire*
Best Supporting Actor: John Gielgud (*Arthur*)
Best Original Screenplay: Colin Welland (*Chariots of Fire*)
Best Costume Design: Milena Canonero (*Chariots of Fire*)
Best Original Score: Vangelis (*Chariots of Fire*)

BAFTA Best Film: *Chariots of Fire*
Best Actress: Meryl Streep (*The French Lieutenant's Woman*)
Best Screenplay: Bill Forsyth (*Gregory's Girl*)
Best Cinematography: Geoffrey Unsworth (*Tess*) (shared)
Best Costume Design: Milena Canonero (*Chariots of Fire*)
Best Sound: Don Sharpe, Ivan Sharrock, Bill Rowe (*The French Lieutenant's Woman*)
Best Original Film Music: Carl Davis (*The French Lieutenant's Woman*)

Berlin –

Cannes Best Screenplay: Jerzy Skolimowski (*Moonlighting*)

1983 Oscars Best Film: *Gandhi*
Best Direction: Richard Attenborough (*Gandhi*)
Best Actor: Ben Kingsley (*Gandhi*)
Best Original Screenplay: John Briley (*Gandhi*)
Best Cinematography: Billy Williams and Ronnie Taylor (*Gandhi*)
Best Art Direction: Stuart Craig, Bob Laing and set decorator Michael Seirto (*Gandhi*)
Best Editing: John Bloom (*Gandhi*)
Best Costume Design: John Mollo and Bhanu Athaiya (*Gandhi*)
Best Live-Action Short: (*A Shocking Accident*)

BAFTA Best Film: (*Gandhi*)
Best Direction: Richard Attenborough (*Gandhi*)
Best Sound: James Guthrie, Eddy Joseph, Clive Winter, Graham Harstone, Nicholas Le Mesurier (*Pink Floyd The Wall*)
Best Actor: Ben Kingsley (*Gandhi*)
Most Promising Newcomer in a Leading Film Role: Ben Kingsley (*Gandhi*)

Berlin Golden Bear: *Ascendancy* (shared)

Cannes Special Jury Prize: *The Meaning of Life*

1984 Oscars –

BAFTA Best Film: *Educating Rita*
Best Direction: Bill Forsyth (*Local Hero*)
Best Adapted Screenplay: Ruth Prawer Jhabvala (*Heat and Dust*)
Best Actress: Julie Walters (*Educating Rita*)
Best Actor: Michael Caine (*Educating Rita*) (shared)
Best Supporting Actor: Denholm Elliott (*Trading Places*)
Most Outstanding Newcomer: Phyllis Logan (*Another Time, Another Place*)

Berlin Best Actor: Albert Finney (*The Dresser*)

Cannes Best Actress: Helen Mirren (*Cal*)
Best Artistic Contribution: Peter Biziou (Cinematography, *Another Country*)

1985 Oscars Best Supporting Actor: Dr. Haing S. Ngor (*The Killing Fields*)
Best Cinematography: Chris Menges (*The Killing Fields*)
Best Editing: Jim Clark (*The Killing Fields*)

BAFTA Best Film: *The Killing Fields*
Best Actor: Dr. Haing S. Ngor (*The Killing Fields*)
Best Actress: Maggie Smith (*A Private Function*)
Best Screenplay Adaptation: Bruce Robinson (*The Killing Fields*)
Best Supporting Actress: Liz Smith (*A Private Function*)
Best Supporting Actor: Denholm Eliott (*A Private Function*)
Most Outstanding Newcomer: Dr. Haing S. Ngor (*The Killing Fields*)
Best Cinematography: Chris Menges (*The Killing Fields*)
Best Production Design: Roy Walker (*The Killing Fields*)
Best Editing: Jim Clark (*The Killing Fields*)
Best Sound: Ian Fuller, Clive Winter, Bill Rowe (*The Killing Fields*)
Best Make-Up: Paul Engelen, Peter Frampton, Rick Baker, Joan Hills (*Greystoke – The Legend of Tarzan, Lord of Apes*)

Berlin Golden Bear: *Wetherby* (shared)

THE BRITISH PICTURE

Films reflect the times
in which they are made,
sometimes deliberately, sometimes
unconsciously. To illustrate this,
some significant events in British
film history are here set in their
historical, political, social and
cultural context.

PART THREE:
THE BRITISH PICTURE

1895 - 1909

1895 Birt Acres uses a 'kinetic lantern' to film the Oxford and Cambridge boat race, the Derby and the opening of the Kiel canal.

The future King George VI is born. H. G. Wells' *The Time Machine* and W. B. Yeats' *Poems* are published. Oscar Wilde brings an unsuccessful libel action against the Marquis of Queensberry.

1896 *The Soldier's Courtship* – Short comedy directed by R. W. Paul about a flirtation on a park bench.

■The French Lumière Brothers give the first commercial film show in London and shortly afterwards R. W. Paul becomes the first Englishman to give a public performance, screening the Derby he has filmed earlier in the day.

Death Of William Morris (poet / artist / socialist) and John E. Millais (painter). First publication of the *Daily Mail*.

1897 *The Twins' Tea-Party* – R. W. Paul's film uses close-ups to show two small children quarrelling.

■The celebration of Queen Victoria's Diamond Jubilee boosts production of newsreels.

Publication of Sidney and Beatrice Webb's *Industrial Democracy* and Havelock Ellis' *Studies on the Psychology of Sex*. Sir Henry Tate gives the Tate Gallery to the British people. The Royal Automobile Club is established.

1898 Double exposure is used as a special effect by pioneer film-maker G. A. Smith.

Death of William Ewart Gladstone and Lewis Carroll. Publication of Thomas Hardy's *Wessex Poems*, H. G. Wells' *The War of the Worlds*, Oscar Wilde's *The Ballad of Reading Gaol* and George Bernard Shaw's *Caesar and Cleopatra*.

1899 One of the effects of the Boer War during the next three years will be rapid development of the newsreel. Birth of director Alfred Hitchcock and Noël Coward (actor / director / writer / composer).

Establishment of London Borough Councils. Publication of Rudyard Kipling's *Stalky and Co* and Oscar Wilde's *The Importance of Being Earnest*.

1900 Cecil M. Hepworth, another pioneer film producer and director makes use of slow-motion photography in his film *The Eccentric Dancer*.

Ramsay MacDonald is appointed secretary of the Labour Party. First publication of the *Daily Express*. Death of Arthur Sullivan (composer), Oscar Wilde (author and dramatist) and John Ruskin (art historian). Elgar's oratorio *The Dream of Gerontius* has its first public performance. W. G. Grace retires from cricket having made 54,000 runs during his career.

1901 *Fire!* – J. A. Williamson's film makes selective use of red tinting and is an early example of editing to combine interior and exterior shots.

■French film-maker and

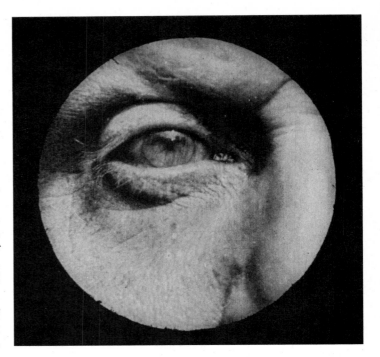

documentarist Charles Pathé establishes a branch in London.

Queen Victoria dies and is succeeded by Edward VII. Rudyard Kipling's *Kim* is published and Elgar's overture *Cockaigne* has its first public performance. The Wigmore Hall, London is opened and boxing is recognised as a legal sport.

1902 Edward VII's coronation is made the subject of many news films. Anthony Asquith (director) is born.

Arthur James Balfour becomes Prime Minister. The Boer War ends with British casualties numbering 5,774. Elgar composes the first of his *Pomp and Circumstance* marches and Edward German's operetta *Merrie England* is performed. Publication of Arthur Conan Doyle's *The Hound of the Baskervilles*, Rudyard Kipling's *Just-So Stories* and Beatrix Potter's *Peter Rabbit* stories. Samuel Butler (author / painter / musician) dies and the *Times Literary Supplement* is published for the first time.

1903 *Alice in Wonderland* – Cecil M. Hepworth's film is photographed in natural settings and uses dissolves between scenes. With sixteen scenes it is one of the longest films of its time. Hepworth's wife plays the White Rabbit.

***The Entente Cordiale* is established with the visits of Edward VII to Paris and Président Loubet to London. Emmeline Pankhurst founds the National Women's Social and Political Union and a 20 m.p.h. speed limit is laid down for motor vehicles.**

1904 *The Mistletoe Bough* – An early horror film about a bride who accidentally becomes incarcerated in a trunk on her wedding day and is never seen alive again.

Drink licensing laws are established and the Rolls Royce company is founded. The Abbey Theatre opens in Dublin and the London Symphony Orchestra gives its first concert. Two leading British writers, Graham Greene and Christopher Isherwood, are born and books published this year include Joseph Conrad's

Nostromo and J. M. Barrie's *Peter Pan*.

1905 *Rescued by Rover* – Directed by Cecil M. Hepworth, featuring his wife (who wrote the story), baby daughter and the first canine star. *Life of Charles Peace* – Directed by William Haggar.

■The first picture house is built from a converted row of shops in Wilton Road, London. It is still standing.

London's first motor buses appear and the Piccadilly and Bakerloo Underground lines are opened. Henry Irving (actor/manager) dies. C. P. Snow (novelist) and Michael Tippett (composer) are born. Thomas Beecham makes his début as a conductor in London. Publication of H. G. Wells' *Kipps* and Baroness Orczy's *The Scarlet Pimpernel*.

1906 The Daily Bioscope, London's first newsreel cinema, is opened at Bishopsgate to show uninterrupted film from noon to 9 p.m. G. A. Smith and Charles Urban patent the first commercially successful colour process for film. Two directors, Carol Reed and Harry Watt, are born.

China and Britain agree to reduce opium production. At 4.5 million London's population is greater than that of New York (4 million), Paris (2.7 million) or Tokyo (1.9 million).

1907 A stage is built at Ealing by Will Barker. It will become the site of the later famous studios (home of the Ealing Comedies from 1948). A number of influential men of the British cinema are born this year: Edgar Anstey, Humphrey Jennings and Paul Rotha (documentarists); Basil Wright (producer/director) and Frank Launder (scenarist).

The United Methodist Church is established and Baden-Powell starts the Boy Scout Movement.

(Left) *Grandma's Reading Glass* (1900), directed by G. A. Smith, was one of the first films to use close-ups. (Below and right) *Rescued by Rover* (1905), directed by Cecil M. Hepworth, featuring his wife and baby daughter.

117

1908 Birth of David Lean, prominent British director (formerly film editor) and Sidney Gilliat (comedy script-writer/director). Two British circuits – Electra Theatres and Biograph – are launched.

H. H. Asquith becomes Prime Minister. The Olympic Games are held in London and the Tiller Girls make their first appearance on the London stage. Lord Northcliffe buys *The Times* and 'Ouida' (novelist) dies. Publication of G. K. Chesterton's *The Man Who Was Thursday*, E. M. Forster's *A Room With A View* and Kenneth Grahame's *The Wind in the Willows*.

1909 *The Tale of the Ark* – Directed by A. Melbourne Cooper.

■The Cinematograph Licensing Act is passed. Provincial Cinematograph Theatres Limited is founded and Glasgow gets its first picture house, the Electric Theatre.

Algernon Swinburne (poet) and George Meredith (novelist) die. The Anglo-Persian Oil Company is established and the Girl Guides are founded. Selfridges department store opens in Oxford Street, London.

The 1910s

1910 *Birth of a Flower* – Percy Smith's first nature film employs his own process – time-lapse photography – to show how a plant grows.

Death of Edward VII, George V succeeds. Thomas Beecham holds his first opera season at Covent Garden. 122,000 telephones are now in use in Britain and the first labour exchanges open.

1911 *Richard III. Wealthy Brother John* – Directed by Bert Haldane.

■In the year of the Sidney Street Siege, Winston Churchill is filmed at the scene. Birth of Robert Hamer (director) and Ronald Neame (cinematographer/director).

Ramsay MacDonald is chairman of the British Labour Party, Winston Churchill is First Lord of the Admiralty. The British Official Secrets Act becomes law and W. S. Gilbert (librettist half of Gilbert and Sullivan) dies. Publication of G. K. Chesterton's *The Innocence of Father Brown* and Katharine Mansfield's *In a German Pension*.

1912 *A Canine Sherlock Holmes* – Directed by Stuart Kinder. *The Reward of Perseverance* – Directed by Bert Haldane. *Oliver Twist* – Directed by Thomas Bentley.

■The British Board of Film Censors is set up. It classifies films according to one of two categories, A and U. London has 400 cinemas.

Miners' strike, London dock strike, transport workers' strike. Captain R. F. Scott reaches the South Pole and the *SS Titanic* sinks on her maiden voyage (1,513 drowned). The Royal Flying Corps is founded (later to become the RAF) and the GPO takes over the telephone system.

1913 *The Fairy Bottle* – Directed by Dave Aylott. *The Great Gold Robbery. Hamlet* – Starring Sir Johnston Forbes-Robertson.

■A newsreel of the Derby captures the death of suffragette Emily Davison who throws herself in front of the King's horse. Henry Cornelius (director) is born.

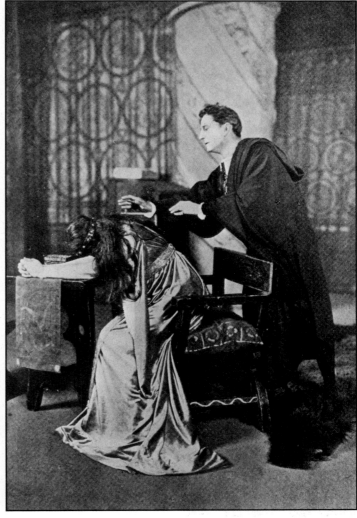

Twickenham film studios, the largest in the country, are opened.

Suffragette demonstrations take place in London and Mrs. Pankhurst is sentenced. The first woman magistrate is sworn in. Sidney and Beatrice Webb start the *New Statesman* and D. H. Lawrence's *Sons and Lovers* is published. Novelist Angus Wilson is born.

1914 *A Study in Scarlet* – Directed by George Pearson. *Trilby* – Directed by Harold Shaw. *The Awakening of Nora.*

■The first animated cartoons to be seen in Britain are made by Lancelot Speed.

World War I and by the end of the year Britain is at war

with Germany, Austria and Turkey. John Tenniel (cartoonist and illustrator of *Alice*) dies.

1915 *Jane Shore* – Directed by Bert Haldane and F. Martin Thornton. *The Prisoner of Zenda* – Directed by George Loane Tucker. *A Welsh Singer* – Starring Edith Evans, her first of two silent film roles.

■Terence Young (director) is born.

London suffers its first zeppelin attack and Ivor Novello writes the wartime song *Keep the Home Fires Burning*. Death of Rupert Brooke (poet), James Keir Hardie (politician) and W. G. Grace (cricketer). Publication of D. H. Lawrence's *The Rainbow*, John

Buchan's *The Thirty-Nine Steps* and Somerset Maugham's *Of Human Bondage*. Lord Beaverbrook buys the *Daily Express*.

1916 *The Man Who Bought London. Comin' Thro' the Rye* – Attended by Queen Alexandra, this Hepworth production is the first film to have a Royal Command Performance.

■Cinema seats are liable to Entertainment Tax. It costs between 4d and 1s (including tea) for a ticket to the pictures.

Lord Kitchener is drowned at sea and the army uses tanks for the first time on the Western Front. Lloyd George is Prime Minister, Beatty is commander-in-chief of the Navy and Jelli-

(Left) *Romance of a Butterfly*, directed by Percy Smith whose nature films used time-lapse photography. (Above) Two scenes from E. Hay Plumb's 'silent' *Hamlet* (1913), which cost the considerable sum of £10,000 to make.

coe is First Sea Lord. Two future Prime Ministers, Harold Wilson and Edward Heath, are born. James Joyce's *A Portrait of the Artist as a Young Man* is published and daylight-saving 'British Summertime' is introduced.

1917 An estimated 20 million people go to the pictures in Britain each week.

Bread is rationed. The British Royal Family renounce their German names and titles. Women 'bob' their hair.

1918 *The Life of Kitchener* – A studio set of the desert in this film is built at the considerable sum of £1,000.

Armistice is signed between the Allies and Germany. There is a General Election resulting in a coalition majority of 262. The poet Wilfred Owen is killed in action on the Western Front. Food shortages lead to rationing and national food kitchens. Women over thirty are given the vote.

1919 *Gamblers All* – Directed by Dave Aylott.

■British Lion is registered as a private company in the Boreham Wood studios.

Peace is celebrated throughout Britain and the first two minutes' silence is observed on the anniversary of Armistice Day. Lady Astor, the first woman MP, is elected and George Curzon succeeds A. J. Balfour as Foreign Secretary. Margot Fonteyn (ballerina) is born. Thomas Hardy's *Collected Poems* are published and Edward Elgar has his first public performance of *Concert in E Minor for Cello*.

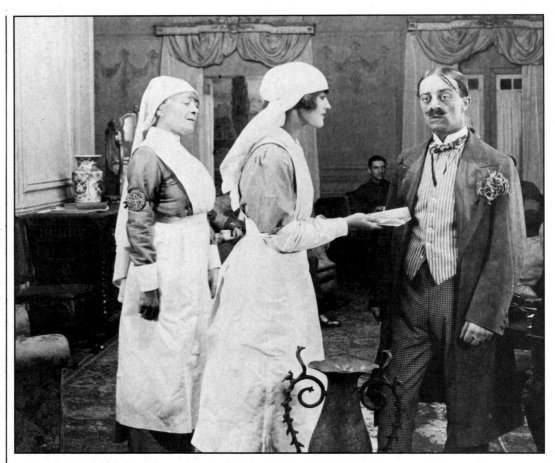

(Left) Two scenes from *Alf's Button* (1920), directed by Cecil M. Hepworth. (Above) *She* (1925), directed by Leander de Cordova.

The 1920s

1920 *Nothing Else Matters* Two darlings of the British cinema, Mabel Poulton and Betty Balfour, play together in their first film. *The Amazing Quest of Mr. Ernest Bliss* – Directed by Henry Edwards. *Anna The Adventuress* and *Alf's Button* – Both directed by Cecil M. Hepworth.

■Alfred Hitchcock is employed in his first film job with Famous Players at Isleworth, writing and designing titles.

Conscription is abolished. Stanley Spencer completes his painting *Christ Carrying the Cross* and Gustav Holst's *The Planets* receives its first public performance. Unemployment Insurance is introduced, 663,000 motor vehicles are licensed, 229 million tons of coal are produced

and 3,747 divorces are granted.

1921 *Moth and Rust* – Directed by Sidney Morgan. *The Fortune of Christina McNab* – Directed by W. P. Kellino.

■Michael Balcon, who is to become a distinguished producer, makes his first film, a documentary. Peter Ustinov (actor / director/ writer) and Jack Clayton (producer/director) are born. Foundation of the British National Film League.

The country estate of Chequers is presented to the nation by Lord Lee and will later become the official country residence of the Prime Minister. John Dunlop, Scottish inventor of the pneumatic tyre, dies. The British Broadcasting Corporation is established and the British Legion is founded. Publication of Aldous Huxley's *Chrome Yellow*,

D. H. Lawrence's *Women in Love* and George Bernard Shaw's play *Heartbreak House*. A total of 7,319 books are published and the population of Great Britain is 42.5 million.

1922 *The Bohemian Girl* – Directed by Harley Knoles. *The Glorious Adventure* – Directed by J. Stuart Blackton.

■420 films are made in Britain this year but fewer than ten of these are sold to the United States. Manchester's Piccadilly Theatre is the first major cinema to be opened in the North of England.

The BBC begins broadcasting. The Liberal Prime Minister Lloyd George is succeeded by Conservative A. Bonar Law. Tutankhamen's tomb at Thebes is discovered by Lord Carnarvon and Howard Carter. The final volume of John Galsworthy's *Forsyte Saga* is published. Other works published this year include T. S. Eliot's *The Wasteland* and Katharine Mansfield's *The Garden Party*. Kingsley Amis (author) is born and George Cadbury (chocolate manufacturer and social reformer) dies. Dr. Marie Stopes holds a meeting in London to advocate birth control.

1923 *The Fair Maid of Perth* – Directed by Edwin Greenwood. *One Arabian Night* – Directed by Sinclair Hill. *Young Lochinvar* – Directed by W. P. Kellino. *Woman to Woman* – This film marks the beginning of the careers of Victor Saville, who directs it, Michael Balcon, who produces it and Alfred Hitchcock, who writes it (and marries the film's editor). American actress Betty Compson is paid £1,000 a week as leading lady.

■British directors Lindsay Anderson and Richard Attenborough are born.

A General Election results in the Conservatives assuming power under Stanley Baldwin. In the year of a London dock strike there are an estimated 4,369,000 trade union members in Britain.

1924 *Decameron Nights* – Directed by Herbert Wilcox. *Another Scandal* – Directed by Edward H. Griffith. *Lovers in Araby* – Directed by Adrian Brunel.

■In the year that Gainsborough Pictures go into film production, the Hepworth Company closes down.

Stanley Baldwin resigns. Ramsay MacDonald forms the first Labour government, but a subsequent general election brings Baldwin back. Winston Churchill, having changed from Liberal to Conservative, becomes Chancellor of the Exchequer. Death of Joseph Conrad (novelist)

and F. H. Bradley (philosopher). British Imperial Airways starts operating flights.

1925 *Confessions* – Directed by W. P. Kellino. *The Rat* – Directed by Graham Cutts. *She* – Directed by Leander de Cordova.

■An estimated 95 per cent of films shown in Britain are of American origin. Film clubs develop including the Film Society in London and the Kinema Club at the University of Cambridge. Professor A. O. Rankine forecasts 'talking pictures'.

Death of Lord Curzon (statesman), Queen Alexandra and H. Rider Haggard (novelist). Austen Chamberlain, the Foreign Secretary, wins the Nobel peace prize. The British Dominions Office is established.

1926 *The Lodger: A Story of the London Fog* – Directed by Alfred Hitchcock. *The Chinese Bungalow* and *Sahara Love* – Directed by Sinclair Hill.

■Film directors John Schlesinger, Bryan Forbes and Karel Reisz, are born this year.

The General Strike lasts nine days but miners do not return to work for six months. Queen Elizabeth II is born. The British Electricity Board is set up and Imperial Chemical Industries (ICI) is formed. Books published include T. E. Lawrence's *The Seven Pillars of Wisdom*, A. A. Milne's *Winnie the Pooh* and G. M. Trevelyan's *History of England*.

1927 *The Vortex* – Written by Noël Coward, directed by Adrian Brunel. *The Ring* – Directed by Alfred

Hitchcock. *Roses of Picardy* – Directed by Maurice Elvey. *Blighty* – Directed by Adrian Brunel.

■Films based on World War I continue to be popular. The Cinematograph Films Act sets a minimum percentage of British films which must be shown in cinemas. Granada Theatres inaugurate regular children's matinées.

General strikes are declared illegal and a union levy is established to provide funds for the Labour Party. Jerome K. Jerome (novelist and dramatist) dies.

1928 *Shooting Stars* – Directed by A. V. Bramble. *You Know What Sailors Are* – Directed by Maurice Elvey. *Champagne* and *The Farmer's Wife* – Directed by Alfred Hitchcock. *Dawn* – Directed by Herbert Wilcox. *The Constant Nymph* – Directed by Adrian Brunel.

■Cinemas opened include the Empire, Leicester Square and the Regal, Marble Arch. Tony Richardson, director of theatre and cinema, is born.

The voting age for women is reduced from thirty to twenty-one. Death of Ellen Terry (actress), H. H. Asquith (Prime Minister 1908-16), Thomas Hardy (novelist) and Emmeline Pankhurst (suffragette leader). John Logie Baird demonstrates colour television and Alexander Fleming discovers penicillin.

1929 *Blackmail* – Written and directed by Alfred Hitchcock, this film, originated as a silent, became the first British 'talkie'. *A Knight in London* – Directed by Lupu Pick. *The Return of the Rat* – Directed by Graham Cutts. *The Lost*

(Left) *The Rat* (1925), directed by Graham Cutts and starring Ivor Novello and Mabel Poulton. (Above) *Boadicea* (1926), directed by Sinclair Hill.

Patrol – Directed by Walter Summers. *High Treason* – Directed by Maurice Elvey.

■Birth of Audrey Hepburn (actress) and John Mortimer (playwright).

After a General Election, Labour is returned with a 26 majority over Conservative. Ramsay MacDonald is Prime Minister. Death of the fifth Earl of Rosebery, who achieved his three aims in life: he married the richest heiress in England; won the Derby (three times) and became Prime Minister (1894-5). Lily Langtry ('Jersey Lily') dies and Stirling Moss (racing driver) is born.

The 1930s

1930 *Rookery Nook* – Directed by Tom Walls. *Murder* – Directed by Alfred Hitchcock. *Harmony Heaven* – Directed by Thomas Bentley. *Raise the Roof* – Directed by Walter Summers.

■Basil Dean (founder of Associated Talking Pictures) and Stephen and Jack Courtauld establish New Ealing Studios. The Comeo-Moulin in Piccadilly becomes the first modern news theatre.

Oswald Mosley resigns from his position in the Labour Government over its unemployment policy. Death of A. J. Balfour (statesman), D. H. Lawrence (novelist and poet) and Arthur Conan Doyle (author). The BBC Symphony Orchestra is formed with Adrian Boult as its musical director. Amy Johnson flies solo from London to Australia in nineteen and a half days.

1931 *Sally in our Alley* – Gracie Fields' first film. *The Skin Game* – Directed by Alfred Hitchcock. *Almost a Divorce* – Directed by Arthur Varney-Serrao. *Tell England* – Directed by Anthony Asquith and Geoffrey Barkas.

■Alexander Korda, Hungarian director and producer who has worked in Hollywood, Berlin and Paris, establishes himself in Britain and founds London Films.

Oswald Mosley leaves the British Labour Party to form his Fascist Party. The issue of unemployment benefits brings down the Labour Government and a National Government is formed. A General Election brings in Ramsay MacDonald as Prime Minister with the National Government winning 558 seats and the Opposition 56 seats. Sterling falls from $4.86 to $3.49.

1932 *Rich and Strange* and *Number Seventeen* – Directed by Alfred Hitchcock. *Rome Express* – Directed by Walter Forde. *Dance Pretty Lady* – Directed by Anthony Asquith. *The Faithful Hearth* – Directed by Victor Saville. *Lord Camber's Ladies* – Directed by Benn W. Levy.

■The passing of the Sunday Entertainments Act enables cinemas to show films on Sundays.

The BBC takes over the development of television from Baird's company. Thomas Hampson sets a world record in his 800-metre run and James Chadwick discovers the neutron. Thomas Beecham founds the London Philharmonic Orchestra and Benjamin Britten composes his *Sinfonietta for Chamber Orchestra, Opus 1*. 2.8 million people are unemployed in Britain.

1933 *The Private Life of Henry VIII* – Directed by Alexander Korda, this historical frolic helps revitalise a declining British Film industry by doing enormously well in the United States. *The Good Companions* and *I Was a Spy* – Directed by Victor Saville. *Orders is Orders* – Directed by Walter Forde. *Bitter Sweet* – Directed by Herbert Wilcox. *Waltz Time* – Directed by William Thiele.

■The British Board of Film Censors add category H (horrific) to their classifications. 169 British films are produced during the year, more than France's 158 or Germany's 127 but considerably fewer than the United States' 547. Foundation of the British Film Institute.

Anglo-German trade pact. George Orwell publishes his *Down and Out in Paris and*

London and James Hilton's *Lost Horizon* is a best seller.

1934 *Evergreen* – Directed by Victor Saville, starring Jessie Matthews. *The Man Who Knew Too Much* (first version) – Directed by Alfred Hitchcock. *The Private Life of Don Juan* – Directed by Alexander Korda. *Death at Broadcasting House* – Directed by Reginald Denham. *Jew Süss* – Directed by Lothar Mendes. *Sing As We Go!* – Directed by Basil Dean. *Blossom Time* – Directed by Paul L. Stein.

■There are 4,300 cinemas in Britain. J. Arthur Rank forms British International Films.

Driving Tests are introduced with the passing of the British Traffic Act and 'cat's eyes' are invented.

1935 *The Scarlet Pimpernel* – Directed by Harold Young, the film adaptation of Baroness Orczy's book stars Leslie Howard. *The Thirty-Nine Steps* – Directed by Alfred Hitchcock. *Mimi* – Directed by Paul L. Stein. *Midshipman Easy* – Directed by Carol Reed. *Me and Marlborough* – Directed by Victor Saville. *The Tunnel* – Directed by Maurice Elvey. *Abdul the Damned* – Directed by Karl Grune. *Turn of the Tide* – Directed by Norman Walker.

■Warner Brothers start producing films at Teddington. The National Film Library (later to become the National Film Archive) is established. Pinewood Studios are opened.

Stanley Baldwin forms a National Government. The British Council is estab-lished. Publication of Walter de la Mare's *Poems 1919 - 1934*, T. S. Eliot's *Murder in the Cathedral* and Sidney and Beatrice Webb's *Soviet Communism: A New Civilisation?*

1936 *Things to Come* – The studio sets used in this film are considered a great technical achievement. Produced by London Films, script by H. G. Wells, music by Arthur Bliss and directed by William Cameron Menzies. *Night Mail* – Documentary film with music by Benjamin Britten and verse by W. H. Auden. *The Ghost Goes West* – René Clair. *Secret Agent* – Directed by Alfred Hitchcock. *The Man Who Could Work Miracles* – Directed by Lothar Mendes. *Rembrandt* – Directed by Alexander Korda.

(Top left) *Sally in our Alley* (1931), Florence Desmond with Gracie Fields who plays Sally Winch, the working class girl with a heart of gold. Directed by Maurice Elvey. (Bottom left) *Things to Come* (1936), directed by William Cameron Menzies. (Below) *The Lady Vanishes* (1938), directed by Alfred Hitchcock seen here on the set of the opening scene with Sally Stewart, Googie Withers and Margaret Lockwood. (Over) *The Four Feathers* (1939), Zoltan Korda directs this triumph of early colour featuring Ralph Richardson.

Idealistic Britons go to Spain to fight in the Civil War. King George V dies and is succeeded by Edward VIII. There is speculation about Edward's relationship with Mrs. Wallis Simpson. Edward abdicates and is made Duke of Windsor, his brother George becomes King. Allen Lane starts his paperback book company, Penguin Books and BBC London begins a television service.

1937 *Sabotage* – Alfred Hitchcock's adaptation of *The Secret Agent* by Joseph Conrad. *Fire Over England* – Directed by William K. Howard. *Knight Without Armour* – Directed by Jacques Feyder. *Victoria the Great* – Directed by Herbert Wilcox. *Good Morning Boys!* and *Oh, Mr. Porter!* – Directed by Marcel Varnel.

■Birth of Vanessa Redgrave, daughter of Sir Michael Redgrave.

George VI is crowned King and the Duke of Windsor marries Mrs. Simpson. The same year the Matrimonial Causes Bill makes divorce easier to obtain in England. Stanley Baldwin retires from his position as Prime Minister and is succeeded by Neville Chamberlain. J. M. Barrie dies and J. R. R. Tolkien's *The Hobbit* is published.

1938 *The Lady Vanishes* – Directed by Alfred Hitchcock. *Bank Holiday* – Directed by Carol Reed. *Pygmalion* – Screenplay by George Bernard Shaw (who wins an Oscar), directed by Anthony Asquith and starring Leslie Howard as Higgins. *The Divorce of Lady X* – Directed by Tim Whelan. *Sixty Glorious Years* – Directed by Herbert Wilcox. *The Drum* – Directed by Zoltan Korda. *The Citadel* – Directed by King Vidor.

In the year of Germany's

invasion of Czechoslovakia, Chamberlain's policy provokes resignations from Eden and from Duff Cooper (First Lord of the Admiralty). Churchill leads the country's protest. Gas masks are issued to British citizens during the Munich crisis. *SS Queen Elizabeth* is launched. Publication of Christopher Isherwood's *Goodbye to Berlin*, Graham Greene's *Brighton Rock* and Daphne du Maurier's *Rebecca*.

1939 *The Stars Look Down* – Directed by Carol Reed, starring Michael Redgrave. *Goodbye Mr. Chips* – Produced by Michael Balcon for MGM's British studio, starring Robert Donat (who wins an Oscar) as the schoolmaster. The film is remade as a musical starring Peter O'Toole in 1969. *French Without Tears* – Directed by Anthony Asquith. *The Four Feathers* – Directed by Zoltan Korda. *Jamaica Inn* – Directed by Alfred Hitchcock.

Britain signs a treaty of mutual assistance with Poland and on 3rd September declares war on Germany. Winston Churchill becomes First Lord of the Admiralty. Conscription is introduced. The first evacuees (women and children) leave London and the song *Hang Out the Washing on the Siegfried Line* becomes popular.

The 1940s

1940 *Gaslight* – Directed by Thorold Dickinson. *The Thief of Baghdad* – Directed by Michael Powell, Ludwig Berger and Tim Whelan. *The Proud Valley* – Directed by Pen Tennyson. *Night Train to Munich* – Directed by Carol Reed.

British Forces are evacuated from Dunkirk and the London Blitz begins. Chamberlain resigns (and dies later in the year). Churchill becomes Prime Minister, and Anthony Eden is Foreign Secretary. Rationing of sugar, butter and bacon is introduced.

1941 *49th Parallel* – Directed by Michael Powell. *Major Barbara* – Directed by Gabriel Pascal. *Dangerous Moonlight* – Directed by Brian Desmond Hurst. *The Farmer's Wife* – Directed by Norman Lee and Leslie Arliss. *Target for Tonight* – Directed by Harry Watt.

■The British Film Producers' Association is formed.

Britain invades Abyssinia, begins its attack in the Western desert, bombs Nuremberg and declares war (with the United States) on Japan. Death of James Joyce, Virginia Woolf and Amy Johnson. Michael Tippett's oratorio *A Child of Our Time* is performed publicly for the first time. Clothes are rationed and 'utility' clothes and furniture are the fashion.

1942 *In Which We Serve* – Directed by David Lean. Noël Coward is largely responsible for the film as writer, composer, producer, co-director and actor. *The Next of Kin* – Thorold Dickinson. *The Foreman Went to France* – Directed by Charles Frend. *Went the Day Well?* – Directed by Alberto Caval-

canti. *The First of the Few* – Directed by Leslie Howard.

The Anglo-Soviet treaty is signed and the Battle of El Alamein begins. The National Loaf is introduced and Tommy Handley's *ITMA* radio show boosts wartime morale. Oxfam is founded (as the Oxford Committee for Famine Relief) and the song *The White Cliffs of Dover* is hugely popular.

1943 *The Life and Death of Colonel Blimp* – Directed by Michael Powell and Emeric Pressburger with Roger Livesey in the leading role. *The Man in Grey* – Directed by Leslie Arliss, starring Margaret Lockwood and James Mason. *Desert Victory* – Directed by Roy Boulting. *We Dive at Dawn* and *The Demi-Paradise* – Directed by Anthony Asquith. *Millions Like Us* – Directed by Frank Launder and Sidney Gilliat.

■R. W. Paul dies and Leslie Howard is killed in an aeroplane crash.

German planes bomb London and the RAF carries out raids on Germany. J. M. Keynes announces his plan for an international currency union which will become the IMF. Death of Beatrice Webb.

1944 *Henry V* – Directed by and starring Laurence Olivier. Music by William Walton. *The Way Ahead* – Directed by Carol Reed. *They Came to a City* – Directed by Basil Dearden. *On Approval* – Directed by Clive Brook. *Champagne Charlie* – Directed by Alberto Cavalcanti. *This Happy Breed* – Directed by David Lean.

D-Day. Troops land in Normandy and the first flying bombs are dropped on London. Books published include H. E. Bates' *Fair Stood the Wind for France* and T. S. Eliot's *Four Quartets*.

1945 *Brief Encounter* – Based on a play by Noël Coward, directed by David Lean, starring Celia Johnson and Trevor Howard. *The Seventh Veil* – Directed by Compton Bennett. *Dead of Night* – Starring Michael Redgrave. *Blithe Spirit* – Directed by David Lean. *The Way to the Stars* – Directed by Anthony Asquith. *The Wicked Lady* – Directed by Leslie Arliss. *Waterloo Road* – Directed by Sidney Gilliat. *I Know Where I'm Going!* – Directed by Michael Powell and Emeric Pressburger.

■330 cinemas are believed to have been destroyed by bombs during the war.

Germany surrenders, VE day is celebrated in Europe, Churchill, Truman and Stalin meet at Potsdam. A General Election brings landslide victory to Labour. **Clement Atlee is Prime Minister. David Lloyd George dies. Evelyn Waugh's *Brideshead Revisited* and George Orwell's *Animal Farm* are published. The Nobel Prize for Medicine is awarded to Fleming, Florey and Chain for discovering penicillin. Family allowances are introduced.**

1946 *Great Expectations* – David Lean's film of Dickens' novel wins an Oscar for its black-and-white photography. *A Matter of Life and Death* – Directed by Michael Powell and Emeric Pressburger. *Caesar and Cleopatra* – Directed by Sidney Gilliat. *London Town* – Directed by Wesley Ruggles.

■Establishment of the British Film Academy. An estimated 31 million cinema attendances are recorded. Laurence Olivier receives an Academy Special Award for his 'outstanding achievement as actor, producer and director of *Henry V*'.

The United Nations General Assembly meets for the first time in London and Churchill gives his 'Iron Curtain' speech. Death of Paul Nash (artist), John Logie Baird (inventor of television) and John Maynard Keynes (economist). The British Arts Council is set up and London Airport begins operations.

1947 *Black Narcissus* – This film about a convent in the Himalayas wins an Academy Award for its use of colour. *Odd Man Out* – Directed by Carol Reed, starring James Mason. *An Ideal Husband* –

(Below) Laurence Olivier as *Henry V* (1944) for which he received an Academy award in 1946 for his 'outstanding achievement as actor, producer and director' of the film.

role. *The Red Shoes* – Starring Moira Shearer, directed by Michael Powell, this film wins an Oscar for its musical score. *The Queen of Spades* – Directed by Thorold Dickinson.

■Foundation of Hammer Films Company.

The British Citizenship Act grants British passports to all Commonwealth citizens. Birth of Prince Charles. W. H. Auden wins the Pulitzer Prize for poetry and T. S. Eliot is awarded the Nobel Prize for literature.

1949 *Kind Hearts and Coronets* – Ealing (black) comedy with Alec Guinness playing all eight victims of a murderous nobleman. *The Third Man* – Directed by Carol Reed, script by Graham Greene. *Passport to Pimlico* – Directed by Henry Cornelius. *The Hasty Heart* – Directed by Vincent Sherman. *Whisky Galore!* – Directed by Alexander Mackendrick. *Stage Fright* – Directed by Alfred Hitchcock.

■Shepherd's Bush studios are sold by Rank to BBC Television. Cinema attendance figures have fallen to 27 million per annum.

George Orwell's *Nineteen Eighty-Four* is published and the Gas industry is nationalised. Clothes rationing ends and Sterling is devalued from \$4·02 to \$2·80.

Directed by Alexander Korda. *Nicholas Nickleby* – Directed by Alberto Cavalcanti. *Frieda* – Directed by Basil Dearden.

■The Dalton Duty – an attempt to boost the British film industry by imposing a tax on imported films – causes bad feeling with the United States which in turn puts an embargo on exports to Britain.

The British Coal Industry is nationalised and Princess Elizabeth marries Philip Mountbatten, Duke of Edinburgh. Death of Stanley Baldwin, Sidney Webb (mathmatician) and A. N. Whitehead (philosopher). A world ground speed record is set up by racing driver John Cobb at 394.196 m.p.h. and hemlines drop with the arrival of the 'New Look' fashion.

1948 *Oliver Twist* – David Lean's Dickens film starring Alec Guinness playing Fagin. *Hamlet* – Laurence Olivier stars and directs in black-and-white and the film wins an Academy Award for costume design. *Scott of the Antarctic* – Directed by Charles Frend and starring John Mills. *The Fallen Idol* – Directed by Carol Reed from a story by Graham Greene with Ralph Richardson in the leading

(Left) Margaret Lockwood is *The Wicked Lady* (1945) directed by Leslie Arliss, based on the novel *The Life and Death of the Wicked Lady Skelton*. (Right) Moira Shearer and shoemaker Leonide Massine in *The Red Shoes* (1948), directed by Michael Powell and Emeric Pressburger.

The 1950s

1950 *Seven Days to Noon* – Directed by John and Roy Boulting. *The Blue Lamp* – Jack Warner's portrayal of the friendly policeman gives rise to the *Dixon of Dock Green* television series. *Odette* – Directed by Herbert Wilcox. *The Happiest Days of Your Life* – Directed by Frank Launder. *The Mudlark* – Directed by Jean Negulesco.

■Category X Certificate is introduced by the British Board of Film Censors. The British Film Production Fund is set up. A voluntary deduction from box-office takings is to be shared between British films according to their earnings. This deduction becomes obligatory in 1957.

A General Election reduces Labour's majority. Britain recognises Communist China and the State of Israel. There is a London dock strike. George Bernard Shaw dies and Bertrand Russell is awarded the Nobel Prize for Literature. London's population numbers 8.3 million and is greater than that of New York (7.8 million) and Tokyo (5.3 million).

1951 *The Tales of Hoffmann* – Directed by Michael Powell and Emeric Pressburger. *The Magic Box* – Directed by John Boulting. *The Browning Version* – Directed by Anthony Asquith. *Laughter in Paradise* – Directed by Mario Zampi. *The Lavender Hill Mob* (Charles Crichton) and *The Man in the White Suit* (Alexander Mackendrick) are two popular Ealing comedies starring Alec Guinness.

■In the year of the Festival of Britain the Telekinema is opened. This will be renamed the National Film Theatre in

1952. Establishment of the Children's Film Foundation.

Diplomats Burgess and Maclean escape to the USSR after being charged with spying. Basil Spence designs the new Coventry Cathedral alongside the ruins of the original one which was devastated by the Blitz. The Conservative Party wins the General Election and Churchill is Prime Minister. Statistics show that 46 per cent of the population works in commerce and industry (as compared with 30 per cent in the United States and 10 per cent in India).

1952 *The Sound Barrier* – Directed by David Lean. *Mandy* – Directed by Alexander Mackendrick. *The Gentle Gunman* – Directed by Basil Dearden and Michael Relph. *The Importance of Being Earnest* – Directed by Anthony Asquith.

■The Telekinema is renamed the National Film Theatre.

King George VI dies and is succeeded by Elizabeth II. Britain produces its first atomic bomb and tests are carried out in Monte Bello Islands, Western Australia. Publication of Samuel Beckett's *Waiting for Godot* and Evelyn Waugh's *Men at Arms*. Agatha Christie's play *The Mousetrap* opens (and is still running). Barbara Hepworth produces her abstract sculpture *Statue* and Lionel Brett designs Hatfield New Town. Trams disappear from the streets of London.

1953 *The Cruel Sea* – Based on Nicholas Monsarrat's novel. *Genevieve* – Directed by Henry Cornelius. *The Titfield Thunderbolt* – Directed by Charles Crichton. *The Maggie* – Directed by Alexander Mackendrick. *The Kidnappers* – Directed by Philip Leacock.

■British directors Cecil

Hepworth and Richard Massingham die.

Coronation of Elizabeth II and Britten's opera *Gloriana* celebrates this first year of a second Elizabethan age. Winston Churchill is awarded the Nobel Prize for Literature and is made a Knight of the Order of the Garter. Edmund Hillary and Sherpa Tenzing (in the John Hunt Expedition) reach the summit of Mount Everest.

1954 *Hobson's Choice* – Directed by David Lean, this third version of the famous stage comedy wins a Golden Bear at the Berlin International Film Festival. *Animal Farm* – Based on George Orwell's allegory, this is Britain's first full-length animated film. *Romeo and Juliet* – Directed by Renato Castellani. *The Belles of St. Trinians* – Directed by Frank Launder. *Knave of Hearts* – Directed by René Clément.

The Independent Television Authority is founded. Roger Bannister runs a mile in 3 minutes 59.4 seconds and Gordon Richards is the first professional jockey to receive a knighthood.

1955 *The Colditz Story* – Directed by Guy Hamilton. *The Ladykillers* – Directed by Alexander Mackendrick, starring Alec Guinness and Peter Sellers. *Richard III* – Directed by and starring Laurence Olivier. *The Dam Busters* – Directed by Michael Anderson.

■There are 4,500 cinemas in Britain.

(Left) *The Blue Lamp* (1950), the film that inspired the *Dixon of Dock Green* television series, directed by Basil Dearden and starring Jack Warner. (Right) *The Belles of St. Trinians* (1954). Headmistress Fritton shows the new games mistress Miss Crawley the St. Trinian's laboratory and tests some of the 'brew' just made, unaware that Miss Crawley is really Ruby Gates, policewoman in disguise, sent to investigate the numerous complaints about the school. (Over) Charles Hawtrey in the first Carry On, *Carry on Sergeant* (1958), directed by Gerald Thomas.

Churchill resigns and is succeeded by Anthony Eden. There are rail and dock strikes. Death of T. E. Lawrence (of Arabia) and Alexander Fleming. J. R. R. Tolkien publishes the first of his three-volume *The Lord of the Rings*. The Duke of Edinburgh announces his award scheme for young people and commercial television goes on the air for the first time.

1956 *A Town Like Alice* – Directed by Jack Lee. *Yield to the Night* – A film about Ruth Ellis, the last woman to be hanged in Britain, made a year after her death. *Reach for the Sky* – Kenneth More portrays disabled war hero Douglas Bader.

■Ealing Studios are sold to the BBC.

Suez Crisis. President Nasser takes over the Suez Canal and Anglo-French forces bomb Egyptian airfields. Anthony Eden rests away from London after the crisis and R. A. Butler acts as Deputy Prime Minister. John Osborne's play *Look Back in Anger* has its first public performance and Colin Wilson's controversial *The Outsider* is published. Bank interest rates are raised to 5.5 per cent, the highest since 1932. Rock and roll becomes popular.

1957 *Woman in a Dressing Gown* – Directed by J. Lee Thompson. *The Bridge on the River Kwai* – Directed by David Lean (who wins an

Academy Award with Alec Guinness, leading role).

■The National Film Theatre moves to the South Bank and hosts the first London Film Festival.

Anthony Eden resigns as Prime Minister, Harold Macmillan takes over. Britain explodes a thermonuclear bomb in the Central Pacific and bank interest rates are raised to 7 per cent.

1958 *Ice Cold In Alex* – Directed by J. Lee Thompson. *The Inn of the Sixth Happiness* – Starring Ingrid Bergman. *Carry on Sergeant* – The first (tame compared to risqué sequels) in the long-running series of comedies.

The 1960s

1960 *Saturday Night and Sunday Morning* – Directed by Karel Reisz, starring Albert Finney. *The Angry Silence* – Bryan Forbes and Richard Attenborough's first co-production. *The Entertainer* – Directed by Tony Richardson. *Tunes of Glory* – Directed by Ronald Neame. *The Trials of Oscar Wilde* (Ken Hughes) and *Oscar Wilde* (Gregory Ratoff) were released in the same year. *Sons and Lovers* – the first of a number of films based on novels by D. H. Lawrence wins an Academy Award for its cinematography.
■Entertainment Duty is abolished. Annual cinema attendances have fallen to 10 million.

Prime Minister Harold Macmillan makes his 'Wind of Change' speech. Prince Andrew is born to Queen Elizabeth (the first birth to a reigning monarch since 1857). There are an estimated 10 million television sets in Britain and 85 million in the United States.

1961 *A Taste of Honey* – Directed by Tony Richardson introducing actress Rita Tushingham. *The Innocents* – Directed by Jack Clayton and based on Henry James' *The Turn of the Screw*. *Whistle Down the Wind* – Directed by Bryan Forbes and starring Hayley Mills.

■One of the earliest news theatres, the Cameo in London, re-opens as the Cameo-Moulin showing continental sex films.

Edward Heath, as Lord Privy Seal, starts negotiating for British entry into the Common Market. Farthings are no longer legal tender.

1962 *The Loneliness of the Long Distance Runner* –

The Campaign for Nuclear Disarmament organises the first protest march to the Atomic Weapons Research Establishment at Aldermaston, and débutantes are presented at Court for the last time. Harold Pinter's play *The Birthday Party* **and Lawrence Durrell's novel** *Balthazar* **are published. Composer Ralph Vaughan Williams dies. Parking meters are introduced.**

1959 *I'm All Right Jack* – Directed by John Boulting, starring Peter Sellers. *The League of Gentlemen* – Directed by Basil Dearden. *Tiger Bay* – starring Hayley Mills. *Look Back in Anger* – Directed by Tony Richardson, based on John Osborne's play. *Our Man in Havana* – Collaboration between Graham Greene (scriptwriter) and Carol Reed (director). *Room at the Top* – Jack Clayton's first feature film, starring Lawrence Harvey.

■G. A. Smith, a pioneer of British cinema, dies at the age of 96.

The General Election brings in the Conservatives with a majority of 100 seats. Viewers watch the progress of the election on their television screens. Death of Stanley Spencer (painter). The M1 motorway is opened.

Directed by Tony Richardson. *Billy Budd* – Directed by Peter Ustinov. *Lawrence of Arabia* – Directed by David Lean (who wins his second Oscar), starring Peter O'Toole. *Dr. No* – First of the James Bond films starring Sean Connery. *A Kind of Loving* – John Schlesinger's first feature film wins a Golden Bear at the Berlin Film Festival.

■ J. Arthur Rank dies.

The Commonwealth Immigrants Act is passed to control immigration to Britain. Thalidomide causes children to be born with malformations. A satirical revue entitled *That Was The Week That Was* is broadcast on BBC television and the *Sunday Times* issues its first colour supplements.

1963 *Tom Jones* – Directed by Tony Richardson. *This Sporting Life* – Lindsay Anderson's first feature secures a prize at the Cannes Festival for actor Richard Harris. *The Servant* – Directed by Joseph Losey. *Billy Liar* – Directed by John Schlesinger.

■ Special Effects cinemas (Cinerama, Circlorama) are opened.

Macmillan resigns as Prime Minister and is succeeded by Alec Douglas-Home. Britain's application to join the Common Market is rejected. Kim Philby is granted asylum in the USSR and Minister Profumo resigns after admitting lying to Parliament over his relationship with Christine Keeler. The Great Train Robbery of the Glasgow-London mail train – thieves get away with £2.5 million.

1964 *It Happened Here* – Kevin Brownlow and Andrew Mollo. *Seance on a Wet Afternoon* – Bryan Forbes. *Dr. Strangelove, or How I Learned to Stop Worrying and Love the Bomb* – Stanley Kubrick's black comedy starring Peter Sellers. *Goldfinger* – The first of director Guy Hamilton's four James Bond films. *Becket* – Starring Peter O'Toole and Richard Burton. *A Hard Day's Night* – The first Beatles film, directed by Richard Lester.

Harold Wilson forms a Labour government and

Winston Churchill makes a final appearance in the House of Commons shortly before his ninetieth birthday. The Windmill Theatre, whose slogan during World War II was 'we never close', closes as a non-stop vaudeville. Violence erupts over Easter between Mods and Rockers on coastal resorts.

1965 *Morgan A Suitable Case for Treatment* – Directed by Karel Reisz. *The Ipcress File* – Directed by Sidney J. Furie. *The Spy Who Came in from the Cold* – Directed by Martin Ritt. *Darling* – Julie Christie in her first major role which wins her an Academy Award, directed by John Schlesinger. *The Knack* – Directed by Richard Lester, awarded a prize at the Cannes Film Festival. *The War Game* – Peter Watkins' film made for BBC television, about the consequences of a nuclear war, is judged too controversial to be shown.

■Nearly 100 cinemas are closed, reducing the total to 1,971.

A year of anniversaries: The seven hundred and fiftieth of Magna Carta; the seven hundredth of Parliament and the nine hundredth of Westminster Abbey. Edward Heath is elected leader of the Conservative party. Winston Churchill and T. S. Eliot die.

1966 *A Man For All Seasons* – Robert Bolt adapts his own play about Sir Thomas More. Directed by Fred Zinnemann, starring Paul Scofield, the film wins a number of Academy Awards. *Alfie* – Starring Michael Caine. *Cul de Sac* – One of three feature films directed by Roman Polanski in Britain wins a Golden Bear at the Berlin International Film Festival. *The Whisperers* – Directed by Bryan Forbes.

Prime Minister Harold Wilson announces a 'wage freeze'. Miniskirts (inspired by designer Mary Quant) come into fashion. The British and Empire boxing champion Henry Cooper is beaten by Cassius Clay (who renames himself Mohammed Ali) but England's soccer team defeats West Germany in the final of the World Cup.

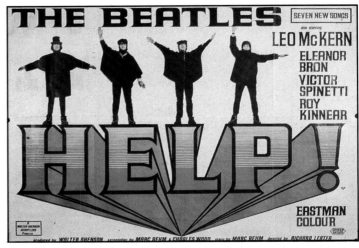

1967 *Accident* – Scripted by Harold Pinter, Joseph Losey's film wins a Special Jury Prize at the Cannes Festival. *The Devil Rides Out* – Directed by Terence Fisher. *Blowup* – Directed by Michelangelo Antonioni. *Far From the Madding Crowd* – Directed by John Schlesinger.

■The British Film Institute establishes its first regional theatres.

Jeremy Thorpe is elected leader of the Liberal Party and Tom Stoppard's play *Rosencrantz and Guildenstern are Dead* **is performed** for the first time. Sandie Shaw wins the Eurovision Song Contest with *Puppet on a string* and Gerry Dorsey changes his name to Englebert Humperdinck. London model Twiggy becomes an international celebrity. Francis Chichester completes his single-handed sailing trip round the world in 225 days.

1968 *Isadora* – Directed by Karel Reisz. *Oliver!* – Directed by Carol Reed, awarded several Oscars. *The Lion in Winter* – Directed by Anthony Harvey. *If . . .* – Winner of the Grand Prize at the Cannes Film Festival, directed by Lindsay Anderson. *2001 – A Space Odyssey* – Directed by Stanley Kubrick. *The Yellow Submarine.*

Death of Anthony Asquith, director. The first John Player lecture is given at the National Film Theatre.

The government restricts immigration from the West Indies, India and Pakistan. Cecil Day-Lewis is made Poet Laureate and Oliver Knussen, aged fifteen, conducts the London Symphony Orchestra in the first public performance of his Symphony No. 1. The government abandons the £55 million project to build a third London airport at Stanstead.

1969 *Kes* – Directed by Ken Loach. *Oh! What a Lovely War* – Directed by Richard Attenborough and adapted from the Joan Littlewood Theatre Workshop production. *The Prime of Miss Jean Brodie* – Oscar awarded to Maggie Smith in the leading role. *Women in Love* – Ken Russell directs from D. H. Lawrence's novel and Glenda Jackson wins an Academy Award.

■The Film Production Board of the British Film Institute records an outstanding year, with British films winning four international prizes. The Cinecenta, housing four separate screens, opens in London's West End. Actor Boris Karloff, star of many American horror films, dies.

Queen Elizabeth invests Prince Charles as Prince of Wales. Samuel Beckett is awarded the Nobel Prize for Literature and The Anglo-French supersonic plane Concorde makes its first test flight.

The 1970s

1970 *The Music Lovers* – A Ken Russell interpretation of Tchaikovsky's life. *Ryan's Daughter* – Directed by David Lean. *Performance* – Directed by Nicholas Roeg – it was rock star Mick Jagger's acting début.

A General Election and a Conservative Government is formed under Edward Heath. Death of E. M. Forster and Bertrand Russell. Publication of C. P. Snow's *Last Things* (the concluding volume of *Strangers and Brothers*) and John Mortimer's *A Voyage Round My Father*. John Galsworthy's *Forsyte Saga* is adapted for television and becomes popular in many parts of the world. Tony Jacklin is the first British golfer to win the US Open Championship in 50 years.

1971 *Macbeth* – Directed by Roman Polanski. *The Boy Friend* – Directed by Ken Russell, starring Twiggy, *A Clockwork Orange* – Stanley Kubrick produces, directs and writes the screenplay based on Anthony Burgess' novel. *The Go-Between* – Harold Pinter adapts the novel by L. P. Hartley, Joseph Losey directs. *Sunday Bloody Sunday* – Directed by John Schlesinger.

■There are disagreements between the British Board of Censors and local councils over the ratings of certain films. John Trevelyan leaves the Board after working on it for twenty years. Charlie Chaplin receives an Honorary Academy Award for 'the incalculable effect he has had in making motion pictures an art form of the twentieth century'. Death of directors Basil Dearden and Seth Holt.

After four hundred years the Church of England and the Roman Catholic Church agree on the 'essential meaning of the eucharist'. A postal strike lasts 47 days. Rolls Royce are declared bankrupt. Decimalised currency is introduced.

1972 *Young Winston* – Directed by Richard Attenborough. *Sleuth* – Directed by Joseph L. Mankiewicz. *O Lucky Man!* – Lindsay Anderson directs, Malcolm McDowell stars. *Family Life* – Ken Loach directs an adaptation of David Mercer's play. *Triple Echo* – First feature of Michael Apted.

■Cinema admissions are 163 million, ten per cent down on the previous year. 89 feature films are made. George Pearson (writer/director/producer) and Dame Margaret Rutherford (actress who played many comic spinsters) die.

Death of Duke of Windsor, Cecil Day-Lewis and Compton Mackenzie (playwright).

1973 *The Hireling* – Alan Bridges' first feature film starring Sarah Miles and Robert Shaw wins the Grand Prize at the Cannes Film Festival. *Don't Look Now* – Thriller directed by Nicholas Roeg and starring Donald Sutherland and Julie Christie.

■74 films are made during the year, of which eight are co-productions with either Italy or France. Cinema admissions are down to 142,250,000. Noël Coward (author / actor/ director / composer / dramatist) and Laurence Harvey (actor) die.

Britain, Ireland and Denmark join the European Economic Commission (EEC). There is an energy crisis, with the Arab oil embargo and general shortage of petroleum products. The Government orders a three-day working week to save energy at the time of the miners' overtime ban.

1974 *Murder on the Orient Express* – Directed by Sidney Lumat. *Mahler* – Directed by Ken Russell. *A Private Enterprise* – Directed by Peter K. Smith.

■For the first time in twenty years cinema admissions have risen (to 143,270,000) but by January 1975 only three major films are shooting in Britain.

After a General Election Harold Wilson becomes Prime Minister for a second time. MP John Stonehouse disappears. Martin Ryle and Antony Hewish are awarded the Nobel Prize for their work in radioastronomy. There is a craze for 'streaking'.

1975 *Tommy* – Ken Russell directs. *Barry Lyndon* – Directed by Stanley Kubrick.

■Disagreement over film censorship continues and complaints are made to both the Greater London Council and the British Board of Film Censors. 46 major films are made during the year, admissions fall to 125,000,000. Charlie Chaplin receives a knighthood. Harold Wilson sets up a working party to investigate the future of British film production which recommends greater investment in the industry.

Margaret Thatcher takes Edward Heath's place as leader of the Conservative Party. Freak weather occurs at various times of the year: it is the mildest winter since 1809, but one night in May is the coldest since records began; snow falls in June, and August sees one day which is the hottest since 1940. The first live radio broadcast of a House of Commons sitting is broadcast. The first shots are fired in the 'cod war' between Britain and Iceland.

1976 *The Man Who Fell to Earth* – Nicholas Roeg directs, David Bowie stars.

(Previous page) Albert Finney in *Saturday Night and Sunday Morning* (1960), directed by Karel Reisz. (Top left) *Help!* (1965), directed by Walter Shenson. (Bottom left) Julie Christie and Alan Bates in *Far From the Madding Crowd* (1967).

MICHAEL DEELEY and BARRY SPIKINGS present for BRITISH LION FILMS
DAVID BOWIE in Nicolas Roeg's film
THE MAN WHO FELL TO EARTH x
Also starring RIP TORN · CANDY CLARK · BUCK HENRY · Produced by MICHAEL DEELEY and BARRY SPIKINGS · Directed by NICOLAS ROEG
Screenplay by PAUL MAYERSBERG from the novel by WALTER TEVIS · Executive Producer SI LITVINOFF · Musical Director JOHN PHILLIPS

Bugsy Malone – Directed by Alan Parker.

■The Association of Independent Film Producers is formed. The film censorship debate continues and the Government intervenes to prevent a Danish director making a film in Britain about the sex life of Jesus Christ.

Harold Wilson resigns, and James Callaghan becomes Prime Minister. Jeremy Thorpe is succeeded as leader of the Liberal Party by David Steel. The summer drought is the worst for 500 years, and Government uses emergency powers to control the water shortage. The first oil is taken from Brent North Sea oilfield.

1977 *Midnight Express* – Directed by Alan Parker, screenplay by Oliver Stone, who wins an Academy Award. *A Bridge Too Far* – Directed by Richard Attenborough. *The Duellists* – Directed by Ridley Scott, winner of a Cannes Film Festival prize.

■Death of Charlie Chaplin.

Death of Anthony Eden and Anthony Crosland. Queen Elizabeth makes a Silver Jubilee tour of Britain. Freddie Laker inaugurates his bargain 'Skytrain' service to New York.

1978 *Stevie* – Directed by Robert Enders. *The Thirty-Nine Steps* – Third version of John Buchan's thriller starring Robert Powell, directed by Don Sharp.

■Box-office takings are up to £217,000,000. Foreign directors and production companies begin to invest again in the British film industry.

IRA bomb attacks strike London, Bristol, Southampton, Manchester and Coventry. Princess Margaret and Lord Snowdon divorce and the world's first 'test-tube baby', Louise Brown, is born. *The Times* **suspends publication for a year due to disagreement over manning levels and new technology.**

1979 *Quadrophenia* – Directed by Franc Roddam and introducing 'Sting'. *Yanks* – Directed by John Schlesinger. *The Bitch* – Starring Joan Collins. *That Sinking Feeling* – Directed by Bill Forsyth.

■The Government allocates an annual sum of £1,500,000 from the Eady Levy. There is a 12 per cent drop in admissions but due to increased ticket prices box-office takings are up.

The General Election brings the Conservative Party to power under Margaret Thatcher, the first woman Prime Minister. Anthony Blunt, art historian, is accused of spying and the *Times* **is published again after being off the newsstands for almost a year.**

The 1980s

1980 *The Tempest* – A controversial adaptation of Shakespeare's play, directed by Derek Jarman. *Gregory's Girl* – Directed by Bill Forsyth. *The Elephant Man* – Starring John Hurt and directed by David Lynch. *The Long Good Friday* – Starring Helen Mirren and Bob Hoskins and directed by John Mackenzie. *Monty Python's Life of Brian* – The Monty Python team's third feature. *The Great Rock 'N' Roll Swindle* – Starring Malcolm McClaren, The Sex Pistols (the group that he managed), and great train robber Ronnie Biggs.

■Alfred Hitchcock receives a knighthood and dies in the same year. Actor Peter Sellers dies. Box-office takings are up to £143,000,000 despite the fact that the number of screens and admissions has fallen.

IRA prisoners in the Maze go on hunger strike. The Iranian embassy siege in London lasts five days and ends when SAS commandos storm the building. Rioting takes place in the St. Paul's area of Bristol. John Lennon is shot dead in New York; Graham Sutherland and C. P. Snow die. Sebastian Coe wins an Olympic gold medal for 1500 metres race.

Unemployment figures are over 2 million.

1981 *Chariots of Fire* – Directed by Hugh Hudson and winner of many Oscars including 'best film', this film is a great international success and heralds a renaissance in the British film industry. *The French Lieutenant's Woman* – Based on John Fowles' novel, screenplay by Harold Pinter, starring Meryl Streep and Jeremy Irons. *Time Bandits* – Directed by Terry Gilliam, animator from Monty Python. *Raise the Titanic* – One of the most spectacular flops in British film history, this film nearly sank the film production career of Lew Grade.

■Despite the international success of British films this year, cinema admissions are down to 86 million and out of 252 films registered in Britain only 32 are made in Britain.

The Social Democratic Party is formed by the 'Gang of Four', Shirley Williams, Roy Jenkins, William Rogers and David Owen. A women's peace camp is established outside Greenham Common air base. Hunger strikers (including MP Bobby Sands) die in the Maze prison. The Prince of Wales marries Lady Diana Spencer. Peter Sutcliffe (the 'Yorkshire Ripper') is arrested for the murder of thirteen women in the North of England.

1982 *Moonlighting* – Directed by Jerzy Skolimowski and starring Jeremy Irons. *The Draughtsman's Contract* – Directed by Peter Greenaway. *Britannia Hospital* – Directed by Lindsay Anderson.

■The inauguration of Channel 4, the first new television channel for eighteen years, is significant for the British film industry for it has a policy of backing independent productions. Kenneth More and Arthur Lowe (of *Dad's Army*) die.

Britain goes to war with Argentina over the Falkland Islands. Unemployment reaches 3 million. Prince William, son of the Prince and Princess of Wales, is born. An intruder is found in the Queen's bedroom and the warship the *Mary Rose* which sank in Tudor times is raised from the seabed.

1983 *Educating Rita* – Directed by Philip Leacock, Julie Walters wins an Oscar. *Local Hero* – Directed by Bill Forsyth, starring Burt Lancaster. *The Ploughman's Lunch* – Directed by Richard Eyre, starring Jonathan Pryce. *Merry Christmas Mr. Lawrence* – An Anglo-Japanese co-production directed by Nagisa Oshima and starring David Bowie. *Gandhi* – It took Richard Attenborough twenty years to bring this award-winning epic to the screen.

■The Monopolies Commission publishes its Report on the Supply of Films for Exhibition in Cinemas. There are 1,327 cinemas in the country. During the year BBC 1 and BBC 2 showed 786 feature films, while ITV showed between 425 and 360. Sir Ralph Richardson, David Niven and John Le Mesurier die.

Margaret Thatcher is returned to power after a General Election. Michael Foot resigns as leader of the Labour Party and is succeeded by Neil Kinnock. David Owen replaces Roy Jenkins as leader of the SDP. Life peerages are granted to Sir Harold Wilson, Jo Grimmond and Gerry Fitt. Lady Donaldson

(Top left) *The Man Who Fell to Earth* **(1976), directed by Nicolas Roeg and starring David Bowie. (Bottom left) David Lynch's** *The Elephant Man* **(1980), with John Hurt in his foam latex make-up that took all day to apply permitting evening shooting only. (Above) Meryl Streep and Jeremy Irons play Sarah Woodruff/Anna and Charles Smithson/Mike in** *The French Lieutenant's Woman,* **screenplay Harold Pinter, from the novel by John Fowles, directed by Karel Reisz (1981).**

(Left) Sir Ralph Richardson's last screen role in *Greystoke: The Legend of Tarzan, Lord of the Apes* (1984), based on the book by Edgar Rice Burroughs and directed by Hugh Hudson. (Top right) John Hurt and Suzanna Hamilton in Michael Radford's *Nineteen Eighty-Four* (1984). (2nd right) Helen Mirren in Pat O'Connor's *Cal* (1984). (3rd right) Colin Firth and Rupert Everett play Tommy Judd and Guy Bennett in Marek Kanievska's *Another Country* (1984). (Bottom right) James Mason in his last screen role, *The Shooting Party* (1985), directed by Alan Bridges.

is elected the first woman Lord Mayor of London. An IRA bomb outside Harrods kills six people and injures many others.

1984 *Nineteen Eighty Four* – Directed by Michael Radford (who also wrote the screenplay from George Orwell's novel), starring John Hurt and Richard Burton in his last screen role. *The Killing Fields* – Directed by Roland Joffé. *The Dresser* – Starring Albert Finney and Tom Courtenay. *Greystoke* – Directed by Hugh Hudson, featuring Ralph Richardson in his last screen role. *The Honorary Consul* – An adaptation of Graham Greene's novel starring Michael Caine and Richard Gere. *Another Country* – Directed by Marek Kanievska and starring Rupert Everett. *Comfort and Joy* – Directed by Bill Forsyth. *The Company of Wolves* – Based on novelist Angela Carter's short stories, directed by Neil Jordan. *Cal* – Screenplay by Bernard McLaverty, directed by Pat O'Connor and starring Helen Mirren.

■The Government publishes its long-awaited White Paper on Film Policy which recommends the abolition of the Eady Levy and the privatisation of the National Film Finance Corporation. At the end of the year the Government introduces its Films Bill, based on the White Paper's recommendations. Cinema admissions are down 10 per cent. James Mason, Richard Burton and Paul Rotha, author of *The Film Till Now*, die.

An IRA bomb attack on the Conservative Party Conference at Brighton kills two MPs and injures many others. There is considerable protest over the imprisonment of Foreign Office clerk Sarah Tisdall for leaking official documents to the *Guardian*.

During the Libyan Embassy seige in London Policewoman Yvonne Fletcher is shot dead. Harold Macmillan receives an Earldom on his eightieth birthday. The miners' strike over pit closures begins.

1985 *A Passage to India* – David Lean's first film since *Ryan's Daughter*, a screen adaptation of E. M. Forster's novel starring Peggy Ashcroft, Alec Guinness and Victor Banerjee. *Brazil* – Directed by Terry Gilliam. *Dance With a Stranger* – Retelling of Ruth Ellis' story, starring newcomer Miranda Richardson and Rupert Everett. Directed by Mike Newell. *Wetherby* – Joint winner of the Golden Bear at the Berlin Film Festival, directed by David Hare, starring Vanessa Redgrave. *The Shooting Party* – Directed by Alan Bridges, starring James Mason in his last role. *A Private Function* – Directed by Malcolm Mowbray.

■The Government publishes its consultative Green Paper on Copyright, which recommends a small levy on the sale of each blank video cassette, as a way of reimbursing copyright holders who are losing money through the criminal activity of home taping. Building begins on The Museum of the Moving Image on the South Bank in London.

British Film Year begins with the twin aims of reawakening the British public's enthusiasm for seeing films in the cinema and of raising the profile of British films and film-makers overseas.

Invited to select what they consider to be the top ten British films of all time, a number of film critics who write regularly for British publications responded with the following choices and comments. The films listed are not necessarily in order of merit; some are simply in alphabetical or chronological order.

ANDY MEDHURST
Brief Encounter (David Lean); *Carry on, Cabby* (Gerald Thomas); *The Cruel Sea* (Charles Frend); *Holiday Camp* (Ken Annakin); *Listen To Britain* (Humphrey Jennings, Stewart McAllister); *Millions Like Us* (Frank Launder, Sidney Gilliat); *Peeping Tom* (Michael Powell); *The Small Back Room* (Michael Powell, Emeric Pressburger); *This Happy Breed* (David Lean); *Victim* (Basil Dearden).

These are in alphabetical order. I've made no pretence of objectivity by choosing 'important' films, although some of my list would also merit that label. Instead I've gone for films I find richly and repeatedly pleasurable. Interestingly, they're all made within a short span of twenty years, which must mean something.

CHRIS PEACHMENT
(Film Editor of Time Out)
Peeping Tom (Michael Powell); *Black Narcissus* (Michael Powell); *Witchfinder General* (Michael Reeves); *The Third Man* (Carol Reed); *Walkabout* (Nicholas Roeg); *The 39 Steps* (Alfred Hitchcock); *The Sound Barrier* (David Lean); *Kind Hearts and Coronets* (Robert Hamer); *The Draughtsman's Contract* (Peter Greenaway); *Nose* (Edmond T. Greville).

The inclination to list ten Michael Powells was only resisted by a sense of fair play.

RICHARD COMBS (Editor of Monthly Film Bulletin)
Barry Lyndon/Lolita (Stanley Kubrick); *The Bed Sitting Room* (Richard Lester); *Blind Date* (Joseph Losey); *The Bridge on the River Kwai* (David Lean); *Cul-de-sac* (Roman Polanski); *Dr. Crippen* (Robert Lynn); *Gone to Earth* (Michael Powell, Emeric Pressburger); *Moonlighting/The Shout* (Jerzy Skolimowski); *Performance* (Nicolas Roeg, Donald Cammell); *Sabotage* (Alfred Hitchcock).

Very much a director's list (there had to be a Hitchcock, a Kubrick, a Lester, a Losey), which avoids those areas thought of as most characteristically English (documentary, horror) to emphasise how much of the best of British cinema has been the creation of non-British directors. Either intentionally or unintentionally, there is something not quite right, reconciled, comfortable or at home about these films.

RACHAEL LOW
The Private Life of Henry VIII (Alexander Korda); *The Man Who Knew Too Much* (Alfred Hitchcock); *Night-mail* (Basil Wright and Harry Watt); *Pygmalion* (Anthony Asquith, Leslie Howard); *In Which We Serve* (Noel Coward, David Lean); *Brief Encounter* (David Lean); *Henry V* (Laurence Oliver); *Odd Man Out* (Carol Reed); *The Bridge on the River Kwai*

(David Lean); *The Killing Fields* (Roland Joffé).

PAM COOK
Black Narcissus (Michael Powell); *Brief Encounter* (David Lean); *Mandy* (Alexander Mackendrick); *The Wicked Lady* (Leslie Arliss); *Saturday Night and Sunday Morning* (Karel Reisz); *Taste the Blood of Dracula* (Peter Sasdy); *Nightcleaners, Riddles of the Sphinx* (Laura Mulvey and Peter Wollen); *The Company of Wolves* (Neil Jordan); *Dance with a Stranger* (Mike Newell).

The films I have chosen show the enormous stylistic diversity of British cinema which is often thought of as uniformly realist and dull.

JAMES PARK
The Red Shoes (Michael Powell); *Peeping Tom* (Michael Powell); *The Third Man* (Carol Reed); *Kind Hearts and Coronets* (Robert Hamer); *Witchfinder General* (Michael Reeves); *Performance* (Nicholas Roeg, Donald Cammell); *The Man Who Fell to Earth* (Nicolas Roeg); *Bill Douglas Trilogy* (Bill Douglas); *Another Time, Another Place* (Michael Radford); *The Draughtsman's Contract* (Peter Greenaway).

Depressing, of course, that so few film-makers have produced an impressive body of work from which to choose a gem or two. But encouraging that four of the above-mentioned directors are very much alive and kicking.

JOHN PYM
(Associate Editor of *Sight & Sound*)
Whisky Galore! (Alexander Mackendrick); *Kind Hearts and Coronets* (Robert Hamer); *The Third Man* (Carol Reed); *Gregory's Girl* (Bill Forsyth); *Bad Timing* (Nicholas Roeg); *The Bill Douglas Trilogy* (Bill Douglas); *I Know Where I'm Going* (Michael Powell, Emeric Pressburger); *Vertical Features Remake* (Peter Greenaway); *Accident* (Joseph Losey); *Caught on a Train* (Peter Duffell).

The last is from television, but to my mind rates as a 'film'.

PHILIP FRENCH
(Film critic *The Observer*; producer Radio-3 *Critics' Forum*).
The Lady Vanishes (Alfred Hitchcock); *The Four Feathers* (Zoltan Korda); *The Life and Death of Colonel Blimp* (Michael Powell and Emeric Pressburger); *Fires Were Started* (Humphrey Jennings); *Henry V* (Laurence Olivier); *Great Expectations* (David Lean); *Kind Hearts and Coronets* (Robert Hamer); *The Third Man* (Carol Reed); *Accident* (Joseph Losey); *Performance* (Donald Cammell and Nicolas Roeg).

The list is chronological, the choice restricted to one film per director. Some of my favourite British directors (e.g. Boorman, Reisz) have done their finest work abroad.

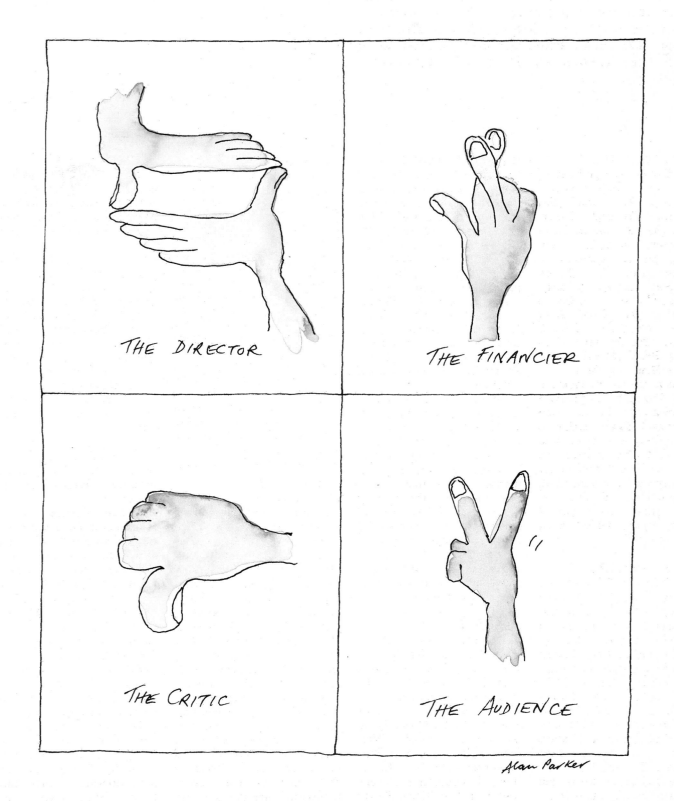

CRITICS' CHOICE

DEREK MALCOLM

The Life And Death Of Colone Blimp (Michael Powell); *Oh Mr Porter!* (Marcel Varnel); *Fires Were Started* (Humphrey Jennings); *The Lady Vanishes* (Alfred Hitchcock); *Great Expectations* (David Lean); *Queen Of Spades* (Thorold Dickinson); *Kind Hearts And Coronets* (Robert Hamer); *The Third Man* (Carol Reed); *Nightmail* (Basil Wright and Harry Watt); *Kes* (Ken Loach).

My only inhibition was self-imposed – one film per director. And I'll admit that distance lends a certain enchantment, so there's nothing more up-to-date than *Kes*. Two I would have much liked to find room for were Gerald Thomas' *Carry On Up The Khyber*, the funniest of the series, and the terrifying *Witchfinder General*, made by Michael Reeves, who died too young to become well-known. Otherwise, the problem was one of selecting one's favourite Hitchcock, Powell, Lean or Reed film. How do you weigh up *Great Expectations* against *Brief Encounter*, or *The Third Man* against the neglected *Outcast Of The Islands*? Twenty favourites would have been much less of a problem.

SASKIA BARON (*City Limits*)

Peeping Tom (Michael Powell; *Black Narcissus* (Michael Powell); *The Long Good Friday* (John Mackenzie); *Performance* (Nicolas Roeg, Donald Cammell); *Kind Hearts and Coronets* (Robert Hamer); *The Servant* (Joseph Losey); *Goldfinger* (Guy Hamilton); *Comfort and Joy* (Bill Forsyth); *Flight to Berlin* (Christopher Petit); *The 39 Steps* (Alfred Hitchcock).

The major drawback is that all the best Hitchcocks were made in America, and I can't remember which of the 'St. Trinian's' films I liked best.

CHARLES BARR

The Manxman (Alfred Hitchcock); *The Faithful Heart* (Victor Saville); *Fires Were Started* (Humphrey Jennings); *A Canterbury Tale* (Michael Powell and Emeric Pressburger); *Brief Encounter* (David Lean); *Mandy* (Alexander Mackendrick); *Hell Drivers* (Cyril Endfield); *Peeping Tom* (Michael Powell);*The Devil Rides Out* (Terence Fisher); *The Golden Vision* (Ken Loach).

Chronological order. To make the exercise more manageable, I've limited myself to one film per director, and, in a rather arbitrary way, one per category (e.g. silent, TV, documentary, Hammer, Ealing). I've cheated slightly by counting Powell and Powell/Pressburger as different filmmakers. *The Golden Vision* is a film made for BBC Television by Ken Loach and Tony Garnett.

TIM PULLEINE

Blackmail (Alfred Hitchcock); *Fires Were Started* (Humphrey Jennings); *The Rake's Progress* (Sidney Gilliat); *The Third Man* (Carol Reed); *Kind Hearts and Coronets* (Robert Hamer); *The Charge of the Light Brigade* (Michael Curtiz); *If . . .* (Lindsay Anderson); *The Bed Sitting Room* (Richard Lester) *The Ploughman's Lunch* (Richard Eyre); *Look Back in Anger* (Tony Richardson).

JILL FORBES

The Third Man (Carol Reed); *Brief Encounter* (David Lean); *Passport to Pimlico* (Karel Reisz); *The Knack . . . And How To Get It* (Richard Lester); *The Thief of Bagdad* (Michael Powell, Ludwig Berger, Tim Whelan); *Blackmail* (Alfred Hitchcock); *Listen to Britain* (Humphrey Jennings, Stewart McAllister); *Gumshoe* (Stephen Frears); *Monty Python's Life of Brian* (Terry Jones).

GEORGE PERRY

The Thirty-Nine Steps (Alfred Hitchcock); *Things to Come* (William Cameron Menzies); *A Canterbury Tale* (Michael Powell, Emeric Pressburger); *Henry V* (Laurence Olivier); *Great Expectations* (David Lean); *It Always Rains on Sunday* (Robert Hamer); *Kind Hearts and Coronets* (Robert Hamer); *The Third Man* (Carol Reed); *Lawrence of Arabia* (David Lean); *The Killing Fields* (Roland Joffé).

I'm aware of the weight being in the 1940s, the lack of a Richardson-Reisz-Anderson-Schlesinger 'new wave' work, and that the choice of *A Canterbury Tale* over *The Red Shoes*, for instance, may seem odd. But this unregarded Powell-Pressburger film in its restored form is a revelation, a most compelling portrait of England in wartime. As for *It Always Rains on Sunday*, it is the precursor of a whole school of television playwriting. *The Third Man* is a great *film noir*, *Lawrence* a breathtaking epic, and *The Killing Fields* an extraordinary fusion of documentary realism and human drama.

NICK RODDICK

Brief Encounter (David Lean); *Odd Man Out* (Carol Reed); *A Diary for Timothy* (Humphrey Jennings); *The Lady Vanishes* (Alfred Hitchcock); *The Servant* (Joseph Losey); *Peeping Tom* (Michael Powell); *Comfort and Joy* (Bill Forsyth); *A Kind of Loving* (John Schlesinger); *The Lavender Hill Mob* (Charles Crichton); *Dracula, Prince of Darkness* (Terence Fisher).

This is not just a list of favourite films (though it is that, too), but a top ten of British films that managed to be cinematically innovative *and* quintessentially British. It was surprisingly easy to do – a comment which, of course, cuts both ways.

JOHN GILLETT Film Research Officer, British Film Institute

Shooting Stars (Anthony Asquith / A. V. Bramble); *Piccadilly* (E. A. Dupont); *The Man Who Knew Too Much* (Alfred Hitchcock) *It's Love Again* (Victor Saville); *The Life And Death Of Colonel Blimp* (Michael Powell and Emeric Pressburger); *Fires Were Started* (Humphrey Jennings); *The Rake's Progress* (Launder and Gilliat); *Great Expectations* (David Lean); *This Sporting Life* (Lindsay Anderson); *The Go-Between* (Joseph Losey).

A very difficult task, of course, but I partially solved it by selecting one film from most of the directors I respond to most. Even so, if one was doing a similar selection in five or ten years time, the directors might be the same but some of the individual titles might be changed.

COLIN McARTHUR

Young and Innocent (Alfred Hitchcock); *Kind Hearts and Coronets* (Robert Hamer); *Peeping Tom* (Michael Powell); *The Criminal* (Joseph Losey); *The Cheviot, the Stag and the Black, Black Oil* (John Mackenzie); *In the Forest* (Phil Mulloy); *Gold Diggers* (Sally Potter); *Crystal Gazing* (Peter Wollen & Laura Mulvey); *Scotch Myths* (Murray Grigor); *Frozen Music* (Mick Eaton).

Why participate in a 'ten best' exercise? The only valid reason is to advance a particular conception of cinema. The conception advanced in the above list is of a cinema (or, more accurately, since some of the titles were made for TV, an audio-visual culture) of stylistic richness, even excess, and social subversiveness, which delights while at the same time calling in question received notions of art and of the world.

TOM MILNE

Peeping Tom (Michael Powell); *Eureka* (Nicholas Roeg); *A Canterbury Tale* (Michael Powell, Emeric Pressburger); *The Man Who Fell to Earth* (Nicholas Roeg); *The Life and Death of Colonel Blimp* (Michael Powell, Emeric Pressburger); *I Know Where I'm Going* (Michael Powell, Emeric Pressburger); *Accident* (Joseph Losey); *The Third Man* (Carol Reed); *A High Wind in Jamaica* (Alexander Mackendrick); *Performance* (Nicholas Roeg and Donald Cammell).

JOEL FINLER

I had originally thought of matching 10 directors and 10 films, but thirties Hitchcock and forties Powell couldn't so easily be dismissed. So here they are – 10 movies, 8 directors: (in chronological order): *The Thirty-Nine steps* (Alfred Hitchcock); *Young and Innocent* (Alfred Hitchcock); *Fires Were Started* (Humphrey Jennings); *The Life & Death of Colonel Blimp* (Michael Powell); *The Red Shoes* (Michael Powell); *Kind Hearts and Coronets* (Robert Hamer); *The Third Man* (Carol Reed); *Bridge on the River Kwai* (David Lean); *Dr Strangelove* (Stanley Kubrick); *The Bed Sitting Room* (Richard Lester).

JOHN COLEMAN
(*New Statesman*)

The Lady Vanishes (Alfred Hitchcock); *Henry V* (Laurence Olivier); *Brief Encounter* (David Lean); *Odd Man Out* (Carol Reed); *Kind Hearts and Coronets* (Robert Hamer); *The Ladykillers* (Alexander Mackendrick); *Saturday Night and Sunday Morning* (Karel Reisz); *Kes* (Ken Loach); *Bleak Moments* (Mike Leigh); *Gregory's Girl* (Bill Forsyth).

My heart bleeds; another 20 or so clamour for inclusion; preponderance of pre-1960 films and just one near-epic (*Henry V*); but I could see/have seen these ten again and again, the test.

GILBERT ADAIR

Fahrenheit 451 (François Truffaut); *Frenzy* (Alfred Hitchcock); *Grown-ups* (Mike Leigh); *A King in New York* (Charles Chaplin); *Man of Aran* (Robert Flaherty); *Modesty Blaise* (Joseph Losey); *Moonlighting* (Skolimowski); *Peeping Tom* (Michael Powell); *Winstanley* (Kevin Brownlow, Andrew Mollo); and, potentially, *I Claudius* (Josef von Sternberg).

VOTES

The ten most chosen films are: *Kind Hearts and Coronets* (Robert Hamer); *Peeping Tom* (Michael Powell); *Brief Encounter* (David Lean); *The Third Man* (Carol Reed); *Fires Were Started* (Humphrey Jennings); *Performance* (Nicholas Roeg, Donald Cammell); *Black Narcissus* (Michael Powell); *The Lady Vanishes* (Alfred Hitchcock); *The Life & Death of Colonel Blimp* (Michael Powell, Emeric Pressburger); *The Thirty-Nine Steps* (Alfred Hitchcock).

BRITISH FILM YEAR
COMMITTEES AND PERSONNEL

Royal Patrons: Their Royal Highnesses The Prince and Princess of Wales

STEERING COMMITTEE
Sir Richard Attenborough (President)
Gary Dartnall – THORN EMI Screen Entertainment Ltd
(Chairman)
James Daly – Rank Film & Television Services Division
Dennis Davidson – Dennis Davidson Associates (DDA)
Clive Parsons – Film & General Productions (until December
1984)
David Puttnam – Enigma Productions (Romaine Hart-Mainline
Pictures, Deputy from March 1985)
John Reiss – THORN EMI Screen Entertainments Ltd. (from
January 1985)
Colin Young – The National Film & Television School

ALL INDUSTRY COMMITTEE
Gary Dartnall (Chairman)
Ian Christie – British Film Institute (BFI)
Fred Cohen – Home Box Office (HBO)
Charles Cooper – Independent Film Distributors
Richard Craven – Eureka Location Management
Jerry Hibbert – The Guild of British Animation
James Higgins – United International Pictures (UIP)
Cyril Howard – Pinewood Studios Ltd
Jeremy Isaacs – Channel 4 Television
Peter King – King Publications Ltd
Edward Lee – Cinematograph Exhibitors' Association of
Great Britain & Ireland (CEA)
James Lee – Goldcrest Films & Television Ltd
Jack Leeming – Post Office & Films Division Department of
Trade & Industry (D.T.I)
Percy Livingstone – Society of Film Distributors Ltd (SFD)
Lester McKellar – Columbia-EMI-Warner Distributors Ltd
Ken Maidment – British Film & Television Producers
Associations Ltd. (BFTPA)
Andrew Mitchell – Elstree Studios
Bill Pay – British Kinematograph, Sound & Television Society
(BKSTS)
David Rose – Channel 4 Television
Sydney Samuelson – Samuelson Group Plc
Alan Sapper – Association of Cinematograph Television & Allied
Technicians (ACTT)
Brian Saunders – Association of Independent Cinemas (AIC)
Martin Schute – British Academy of Film & Television Arts
(BAFTA)
Douglas Thomas – The Cinema Advertising Association (CAA)
John Wilson – National Association of Theatrical Television &
Kine Employees (NATKE)

FINANCE & GENERAL PURPOSES COMMITTEE
Clive Parsons (Chairman, until December 1984)
John Reiss – (Chairman, from January, 1985)
George W. Eccles – Deloitte, Haskins & Sells
Bernard Kingham – Deputy Chief Executive – ITC Entertainment
Marc Samuelson – Association of Independent Producers
R. A. Storer – Harbottle & Lewis

EDUCATION & INFORMATION COMMITTEE
Colin Young – (Chairman)
John Brown – Scottish Film Council
Jo Bussey – THORN EMI Screen Entertainment Ltd.
John Chittock – Screen Digest
Andy Egan – ACTT
Chris Goodwin – Journalist
Gillian Hartnoll – BFI Library
John Howkins – International Institute of Communications
Wolf Rilla – Directors Guild of Great Britain
Prof. Richard Ross – School of Film & Television Royal College
of Art
David Samuelson

Education & Information Committee (cont.)
Marc Samuelson – Association of Independent Producers (AIP)
Philip Simpson – BFI Education
Colin Vaines – National Film Development Fund (NFDF)
Peter Scott – Film Publicist

INTERNATIONAL EVENTS COMMITTEE
Dennis Davidson – (Chairman)
Robert Bingham – Button Design Contracts Ltd
Malcolm Cockren – Bayley, Martin, Fay Entertainments Limited
Gerry Lewis – UIP
Brian Humphreys/Bruce Nightingale – The British Council
Greg Smith – Euston Films
Keith Turner – Virgin Films

NATIONAL EVENTS COMMITTEE
David Puttnam – (Chairman)
Carolyn Keen – Information/Publicity Co-ordinator
Tim Bell – Lowe Howard-Spink Campbell-Ewald
Ray Connolly – Writer
Romaine Hart – Mainline Pictures
Gilly Hodson – Dennis Davidson Associates (DDA)
Barry Jenkins – Cannon Classic Cinemas Ltd
Joanna Lumley – Actress
Derek Malcolm – The Guardian
Lynda Myles – Producer
Philip Nugus – National Video Corporation
Peter Plouviez – British Actor's Equity Association
Anthony Smith – British Film Institute (BFI)
Lynda Smith
Martin Stafford – THORN EMI Screen Entertainment Ltd.

PUBLICITY COMMITTEE
Dennis Davidson – (Chairman)
Denis Cave – PIC
Duncan Clark – UIP
Mundy Ellis – British Film Institute (BFI)
John Grundy – Downton Advertising
Diana Hawkins – Diana Hawkins Publicity
Gilly Hodson – Dennis Davidson Associates (DDA)
Nick Kent – Stills Magazine

BRITISH FILM YEAR PERSONNEL
Fiona Halton – Executive Director
Keith Howes – Consultative Director
Cheryl Gillan – International/Special Events Manager
Philip Astell – Financial Controller
Ian Wall – Education Officer
Nicola Hervey – National Events Organiser
Wendy Robinson – National Events Organiser
Stephanie Wilson – National Events Manager
Gillian Dobias – International Events Organiser
Romaine Hart (Chairman from March, 1985)
Valerie Blackborn – Office Manager
Jane Arthurs – National Events Administrator
Sharon Burns – Information/Publicity Assistant
Shelagh Donlevy – Education Co-ordinator
Nicole Emberson – National Events Administrator
Carol Hammond – Wordprocessor Operator
Bunny King – Reception
Vivienne Sasson – Competition Co-ordinator
Angela Walkes – National Events Secretary
Valerie Blackborn – Office Manager
Jacqui Land – National Events Secretary